C-130
Hercules
in action

by Lou Drendel

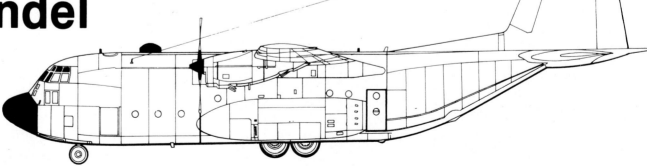

squadron/signal publications

AC-130A, 54-1623, as it appeared during deployment to Ubon RTAB, 1970-71. Ghost Rider survived the war and was with the 711th SOS, 919th SOG at Duke Field, Florida (Eglin Aux #3) in 1980. Other named AC-130s which did not survive included War Lord (54-1625) shot down over the Ho Chi Minh Trail in April 1970, Prometheus (55-044) shot down southeast of Tchepone, Laos, March 1972, and Thor (56-0490) shot down over An Loc, December 1972.

ISBN 0-89747-111-3

If you have any photographs of the aircraft, armor, soldiers or ships of any nation, particularly wartime snapshots, why not share them with us and help make Squadron/Signal's books all the more interesting and complete in the future. Any photograph sent to us will be copied and the original returned. The donor will be fully credited for any photos used. Please send them to: Squadron/Signal Publications, Inc., 1115 Crowley Dr., Carrollton, TX 75006.

Photo Credits

Lockheed
USAF
USN
USMC
Norman E. Taylor
Dave Davenport
Paul Stevens
Charles Mayer
Jerry Geer
D. Kasulka
S. Peltz
R. Archer
RCAF

Other *in Action* Titles
by Lou Drendel

F-4 Phantom	A-7 Corsair II
F-8 Crusader	B-52
F-100 Super Sabre	F-15 Eagle
A-4 Skyhawk	F-104 Starfighter
Gunslingers	B-47
F-106 Delta Dart	F-14 Tomcat
F-105 Thunderchief	F-111
A-6 Intruder	F-5

Introduction

"26 October, 1956 — Jump Number 16 — Service Company, 325th Airborne Infantry Regiment, 82nd Airborne Division — Drop Zone Sicily, Fort Bragg, N.C. — Stick Position, 20 — Parachute Type, T-10 — Type Jump, Combat Equipment — Type Aircraft, C-130 — Remarks; "Impressive Airplane!""

This entry from my Jump Log, now almost a quarter century old, its pages yellowing and dog-eared, describes my introduction to the C-130. At the time, I had been in the Army just a year and I was thoroughly enjoying jumping out of airplanes. I volunteered for every jump that came up. Since this was the era of the peacetime Army, the 82nd was far understrength and there were lots of opportunities to jump. When the chance to blast a new airplane came along, I couldn't resist. The jump was arranged through the auspices of the Continental Army Command's Test Board Five and, to the best of my knowledge, it was the first time that paratroops were to be dropped from the C-130. Major Russ Dobyns, one of the Air Force Test Pilots in the 130 program, brought the airplane up to Pope AFB from Marietta for the tests. We had manifested a full load of 64 parachutists, as well as 5 observers from the Test Board.

I should say a word about the "Impressive Airplane!" remark I recorded in my Jump Log. Until that flight, I had had exactly 24 airplane rides, fifteen of which were terminated in mid-air. The most impressive airplane I had flown in was probably the Constellation. All of my previous experience with Air Force aircraft had been limited to the C-119 Flying Boxcar. If you have ever flown in the C-119, you will immediately understand how an Army Private, with limited flying experience, could be moved to comment enthusiastically on the performance of the C-130. The C-119 was a follow-on to the C-82 Packet. It entered production in 1949, a total of 1,112 being built, several of which are flying missions today. It was the backbone of the medium tactical transport force in 1956 but it was severely limited in several categories. (A popular story of the day insisted that scientific analysis proved that neither the bumblebee nor the C-119 would fly at all!) The Flying Boxcar (a name which didn't help its aerodynamic reputation much) did take a lot of concrete to get airborne and was no heavyweight lifter. The Air Force Heavyweights, the C-54 and C-124 were slow in the air, and slow to turn around, once on the ground. This had been demonstrated painfully at the beginning of the Korean War. That war, fought on the other side of the globe, demonstrated the necessity for a modernization of the strategic and tactical airlift forces. A good deal of thought was put into writing the specifications for the new transports. Yes, plural transports. The Air Force put out Requests for Proposals on 3 new transports in 1951 and 1952. The General Operating Requirements specified in the C-130 RFP were written to encompass four missions. The resupply mission required a payload of 37,800 lbs, carried out to 950 nautical miles and return without refuelling. The airhead mission specified resupply of troops in the combat zone and required a payload of 25,000 lbs, carried for 1,100 at low level and high speed and return without refuelling. The troop carrier mission called for carrying 92 combat-equipped infantrymen, or 64 parachutists. The logistic support mission required a payload of 37,800 lbs, carried for a range of 1,700.

The industry was well aware of Pentagon thinking and the competition for the new transport contract was stiff. Designs were submitted by Fairchild, Boeing, Lockheed and Douglas. Lockheed's competitors all had recent experience in building transport aircraft. The closest thing to a transport type that Lockheed had built was the sleek Constellation, which, though adapted for the military role, was really a plush long-range airliner. But if Lockheed was short on practical airlift experience, it was long on innovative design thought and its winning proposal exhibited pure genius. The general layout of the C-130

An early production C-130A demonstrates its maneuverability on a test flight out of Lockheed's Marietta Plant. The effectiveness of the controls so necessary for low speed handling on approaches and departures from rough, unimproved fields turned many C-130 drivers into quasi-fighter jocks. (Lockheed)

The second prototype YC-130 on an early flight from Burbank. The two prototypes were built at Burbank, with all production since that time having been shifted to Marietta. (Lockheed)

is pretty much taken for granted today, as all the best airlifters have imitated the basic Hercules configuration, but when the wraps came off in 1952, its appearance shocked and dismayed many aviation people, who had come to expect innovation in the form of swept-back or slimmed-down. But pretty is as pretty does and the Herk began winning advocates on its first flight on August 23, 1954. It is still winning converts today.

As I recall it, my first sight of the C-130 that day in 1956 did not produce any great shock. We didn't much care what it looked like, as long as it got us to the drop zone without any problems. If I had been more knowledgeable about airplanes, I might have been impressed with the fact that the landing gear seemed to have been stuck onto the fuselage sides as an afterthought. This kept the cargo compartment from getting cluttered up. Then too, the four main gear wheels were mounted in tandem, an ingenious layout that made for better performance on unprepared fields. (The leading tire would plow a path for its follower.) Since we didn't expect to be flying in the stratosphere, I probably wouldn't have been impressed with the fact that the cavernous fuselage, with all its doors and windows, was fully pressurized,...no mean feat, and very necessary for those long flights, since altitude means range with a jet engine. We were impressed with the big cargo loading ramp at the rear of the airplane, which was situated conveniently at truck-bed height when dropped to a level position. It could be dropped further and, with the addition of a couple of short ramps, you could drive your truck right aboard! If I had been a pilot and had been allowed to visit the flight deck, I would surely have been impressed with the layout of the controls and the absolutely amazing visibility afforded by all those windows in the nose. (Pilots continue to be impressed and amazed today).

During our pre-flight briefing, we were shown the prop-blast deflectors that would pop out of the rear of the wheel well fairings, allowing us to leap off the step that was extend-

ed straight out the door from the floor of the cabin. The C-130 fuselage is much rounder in cross-section than that of the C-119, resulting in a door threshold that is further inboard than the center of door. The extendable platform allowed us to get our knees in the breeze before we jumped. It also allowed us to depart the airplane more easily. That round fuselage had been flattened at the top to accomodate the wing carry-through box, and at the bottom to create a flat floor. Its dimensions (10 feet wide, 9 feet high, and 41 feet long) were those of a standard railroad boxcar.

When Russ Dobyns fired up those four Allison T-56A Turboprops, the noise was deafening. Even with the doors closed, there was no way to carry on normal conversation. This was before the era of commercial jet aviation and the only turboprops plying the airways at that time were those of the British Viscount, which most of us had yet to see, hear or ride in. We were impressed with the noise, even if we didn't understand the principle behind the constant high rpm (13,820 for the turbine, 1,106 for the prop). Those four turboprops were one of the most impressive features of the C-130. They produced 3,750 equivalent shaft horsepower each, which added up to a power-to-weight ratio of 2.3 per Lb. That gave the Herk a cruising speed of 360 and, with the acceleration of a prop, would allow operations out of short fields. The prop was reversible, which allowed for landings as well on short fields. Add to that the reliability factor of the jet engine, which had many fewer parts than the recip, and you had incontestible evidence of the superiority of the jet engine. That reliability added up to a higher utilization rate, which coupled with the higher load factors, put the final nail in the C-119's coffin. The Hercules would turn out to be 50% cheaper to operate than the C-119 on an hourly basis.

If we were impressed with the noise of the C-130, we were absolutely astounded by the tremendous acceleration it demonstrated on takeoff. All of a sudden, we were leaning to the rear, in unison, at a 45 degree angle! (You sit sideways.)The looks on our faces were all variations of astonishment! This was the kind of demonstration that couldn't fail to impress you, whether you were on the flight deck or huddled in the hold. It was one of the reasons that pilots fell in love with the Hercules from that first flight. It has more power

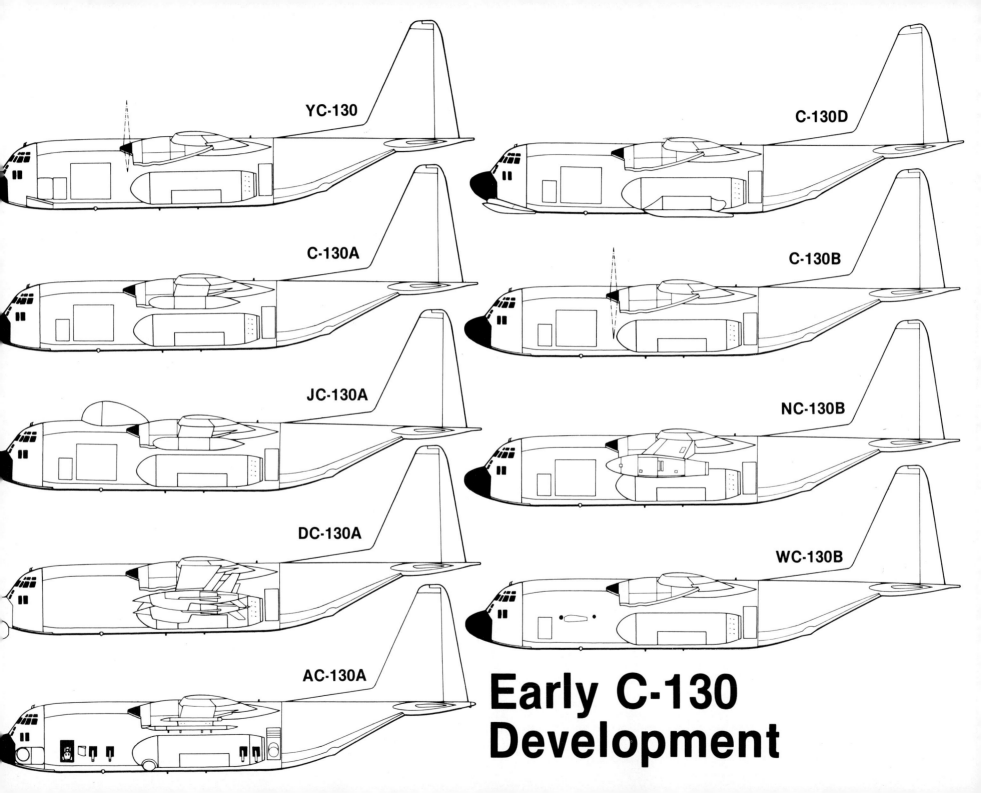

YC-130

C-130A

JC-130A

DC-130A

AC-130A

C-130D

C-130B

NC-130B

WC-130B

Early C-130
Development

than you think you have a right to expect from a transport. Add to that power the maneuverability and handling ease afforded by the hydraulically-boosted controls and you can see why the C-130 began turning transport pilots into fighter pilots from the moment they got their hands on the controls. In fact, the first wing to receive the C-130 formed an airshow team. The 463rd Troop Carrier Wing, which received their 130s in December 1956 fielded the "Four Horsemen". The Horsemen flew regular wing airplanes for the airshow routine, which included a diamond formation, arrowhead and echelon. They even demonstrated maneuvers such as a bomb-burst. The formation they flew was close and precise, eliciting expressions of admiration, or disbelief, from fighter pilots.

Our ride to the drop zone was all too short. It seemed we had barely leveled off when the red light came on, signalling 6 minutes until we jumped. The Jumpmaster stood up and began to intone the jump commands over the loudspeaker system. This was another innovation that was felt to be necessary because of the size of the airplane. In the smaller C-119, only four minutes were required for the jump commands. In the 130 we had to stand up one stick at a time, fold our seats, then wait until the other sticks stood and folded their seats before continuing with the procedure. They had allowed us an extra two minutes for this and it seemed to work quite adequately. They had also selected the longest Drop Zone at Fort Bragg for our jump. Sicily is about forty seconds long, though it is divided in the middle by a narrow waist. We had 32 jumpers on each side of the airplane, which gave us over a second a jumper to get out. (This was more than enough time. A planeload of 82nd jumpers had emptied the 40 seat C-119 in something under 10 seconds!) Any worries we might have had about fighting our way out the door in the face of that fierce turboprop blast proved to be groundless. With the airplane slowed to 120 knots, the flaps down and the blast deflectors out, getting out the door and clear of the fuselage was a piece of cake. Once out the door, it was all the same, one second the sound and fury of flight in a powerful airplane at 140 miles per hour, then the rustle and snap of your parachute opening, then the seemingly unearthly quiet with only the gentle soughing of the wind through the suspension lines, punctuated by the occasional panicky admonition of one of your fellow troopers to "SLIP, SLIP!" as canopies drifted into one another. In less than a minute we were on the ground. The general consensus was favorable. Here was an airplane in which you felt safe and comfortable and from which, though not as easy to get out of as the Dollar Nineteen, it was easy enough to jump. (Because of its bullet shaped rear end, the C-119's jump doors were slightly canted inward, and allowed you to fairly run right out the back end. This is what led to the record-breaking pace of exit from the 119. It also led to lots of entanglements in the air and, believe me, there is nothing in the world anymore exciting than landing atop another parachute a thousand feet in the air, with your own canopy robbed of its air and collapsing around you, and having to walk off, knee deep in nylon, hoping that your parachute will re-inflate!)

Unfortunately, Russ Dobyns' return to Pope was not as uneventful as our flight out had been. Arriving in the traffic pattern, he selected gear down, and nothing happened. A bushing had failed on the landing gear's jack screw and was stuck so tight that even the 3,000 pounds per square inch pressure of the hydraulics would not budge it. A direct patch-through to Dick Pulver, Lockheed's chief engineer, who was in Marietta, resulted in a lot of conversation and alternative methods for getting the gear down, all to no avail. The five Army Colonels from the Test Board were probably wondering about the wisdom of coming along on this flight without their parachutes but, for the record, they stated their confidence in the airplane. Dobyns flew around, burning off fuel, while the crash crew at Pope prepared for his arrival. The runway having been foamed and with just enough fuel for the landing, he set up on a long final. Seconds from touchdown, the wind shifted 180 degrees and the tower advised him to go around. Murphy's law upheld! As is so often the case in emergency situations, totally unrelated events seem to conspire to aggravate the original problem. Russ flew one of the tightest patterns seen at Pope and got it on the ground with all four engines turning. The landing was a pure grease job, the Herk skidded about 1200 feet before coming to a stop on the centerline. A lot of skin was shed in a shower of spectacular sparks and all the antennas were ground off, but the damage was limited to the outside. The airplane was repaired sufficiently for the trip back to Marietta

by the next day. As dramatic as this was, we knew nothing about it and I had to wait until twenty-four years later to find out about the impressive return to Pope of the "Impressive Plane". My jump log shows that I had a further five jumps from the C-130. By the time I went through Jumpmaster School, in early 1958, the 130 was fully integrated into the tactical airlift forces. It had changed the concept of the Composite Air Strike Force from wishful thinking to reality. With the C-130, the United States acheived global reach with its quick reaction forces. The changes this brought were swift and marked. The easy-going peacetime Army of 1956 and early 1957 disappeared under an avalanche of reorganization and the 130 airlifted CASF forces to Lebanon in 1958. Its record in the intervening years has been one long, unbroken string of successes, in military, humanitarian and commercial endeavors.

Troopers of the 82nd Airborne demonstrate the troop carrier accomodations of the C-130. For the purpose of this publicity shot, they are wearing Air Force parachutes, with no chestpack reserve chute and no combat equipment. (Lockheed)

C-130A

Though the two YC-130 prototypes were built at Lockheed's Burbank, California plant, production of all subsequent models was to take place at Lockheed-Georgia. The Lockheed plant at Marietta, Georgia is the largest of its kind in the world. It had been built during World War II and operated by Bell, which built B-29s under license from Boeing. At the conclusion of the war it was turned into a storage facility, only to be reopened by Lockheed in 1951 after they had received a contract to refurbish mothballed B-29s for the war in Korea. Lockheed also received a contract to manufacture B-47s under license. The Georgia Division's performance on this contract, in which 394 B-47s were built, resulted in the return to DoD of several million dollars in allocated defense funds. This was an unheard of event, before or since, and Lockheed executives were itching to get a contract for their super-efficient Georgia division. The award of the C-130 contract to Lockheed in 1952 ensured continued operation of the Marietta plant, though at the time no one imagined that it would still be producing C-130s 28 years later! (Company officials indicated that they would have been happy with a production run of 300 airplanes.)

The first production C-130 was rolled out of the Marietta plant on March 10, 1955. It made its first flight on April 7, immediately gaining the awestruck advocacy of everyone who watched that first departure. Test pilots Bud Martin and Leo Sullivan had it off the ground within 800 feet, crossing the departure end of the 10,000 foot runway with 2,500 feet of altitude!

There was just one major problem with the initial production Hercules. The three bladed Curtiss-Wright electric propellers refused to perform consistently. The T-56 engine is a constant speed engine which transmits its power through the props, which must act as transmissions with an infinite number of gearings, by means of controllable blade pitch. Pitch changes were electrically activated which always seemed to cause too much change, one way or another. Finally, one of the test airplanes was fitted with hydraulically-operated Aero-Products three-bladed props. These performed so consistently that all efforts to fix the electric props were dropped and the hydraulic model was adopted. The Air Force initiated a competition to determine which props would be used on future production C-130s. The winner was a four-bladed Hamilton-Standard hydraulic, which has been the standard prop for all 130s from the B model onwards. While the propeller problem persisted, it caused a backup in the delivery of C-130s. This gave Lockheed a chance to identify and correct dozens of minor glitches that would otherwise have had to have been dealt with in the field. The result was an enhanced reliability record for the Herk when it entered service, beginning in December 1956.

C-130A of the 463rd TCW at Hickam AFB stopover enroute to Ashiya AB, Japan, where the 463rd was based in the late fifties. (Derek Mau)

C-130A of the 317th Troop Carrier Wing, out of Lockbourne AFB, on approach to RAF Mildenhall, 1966. This aircraft was eventually given to the ill-fated South Vietnamese Air Force. (P. Bennett via R. Archer)

Early 'A' Nose

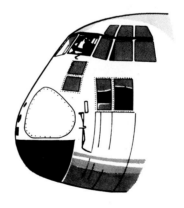

Later 'A' Nose

C-130D-50-LM of the 139th TAS, New York ANG at RAF Greenham Common for the big anniversary party thrown for the Herk in June 1979. First ski evaluations took place at Bemidji Lake, Minnesota in February 1957. The Ski Herk set a record for ski-equipped airlifters of 124,000 pounds the following February at Bemidji. The twenty foot long main skis weigh in at one ton apiece, and both nose and main skis will pitch up 8 degrees and down 15 degrees to accomodate landings on rough terrain. (H. Scharringa via N.E. Taylor)

The first C-130 to be equipped with skis made its initial flight on January 29, 1957. A television camera was mounted under the right wing, outboard of the engines. The closed-circuit picture was viewed by Lockheed test engineers in the cargo compartment during the 51 minute first flight. This aircraft was later acquired by the U.S. Navy and re-serialled 158228. (Lockheed via C.B. Mayer)

The number five C-130A was initially delivered to the 3206th Test Wing at Eglin AFB, Florida in January 1956. It was later modified to JC-130A configuration and served at Hanscom Field in the Weather Research (Cloud Physics) role. Later still, it was modified to NC-130A standard and finally finished its career in 1978, with retirement to the boneyard at Davis Monthan AFB. (via Grant Matsuoka)

In the course of a long and distinguished test career, 53-3133 carried a variety of equipment and color schemes, including, in the early days, an Arctic Red tail and International Orange nose and, later on, the white upper and natural metal lower surfaces seen in these three shots. (via Grant Matsuoka)

NC-130A of the 4950th Test Wing, Aeronautical Systems Division, Wright Patterson AFB, Ohio, July 1976. (Dave Menard via Paul Stevens)

The same aircraft seen above ten years earlier, identified in this photo as a JC-130A, while working out of L.G. Hanscom Field. (via Paul Stevens)

JC-130A of the 4950th Test Wing as it appeared in May 1963 during an appearance at Friendship International Airport in Baltimore. "Local Yokel" carries the badge of the Air Force Systems Command and is configured for satellite retrieval duty. (via Paul Stevens)

54-1632 was the prototype TC-130A and, later, the prototype RC-130A. It is seen here in the latter configuration, while assigned to the 1370th Photo Mapping Wing. Tail band initials signify Aerial Cartographic and Geodetic Survey. Airplane later served with the 706th and 704th TASs before being retired to MASDC in 1978. (Fred Roos via C.B. Mayer)

RC-130A of the 1st ACGS at Forbes AFB, May, 1968. This aircraft later converted to straight C-130A and served with the 143rd TAS into the later '70s. (Jerry Geer)

The RC-130S is equipped with BIAS (Battlefield Illumination Airborne System) in twin pods carried ahead of the landing gear fairings. The pods carry 28 lamps, which produce a combined 6.14 million candlepower. It carries a crew of six, including, pilot, co-pilot, navigator, engineer and two illuminators. (Jim Sullivan)

DC-130A of the 11th TAC Drone
Squadron, 355th TFW, Davis Monthan
AFB, as it appeared in November
1971. The DC-130 is used as a launch
and command transport for a variety
of aeronautical drones, including
reconnaissance, electronic in-
telligence, strike and targets. (Dave
Menard via Norm Taylor)

U.S. AIR FORCE

TV 16

Ryan Firebee

54-1626 served as the prototype AC-130A, while assigned to the 4950th Test Wing, Wright-Patterson AFB, OH, 1966-67. It was shot down over Vietnam in March 1972. (Grant Matsuoka)

It was still assigned to the 4950th in 1971, though it had received the modified radome when seen here on a flight out of Patuxent River NATC during initial testing of the 105mm gun. Originally designated "Gunship II" (The AC-47 was Gunship I), the AC-130A was put together from leftovers, tested at Eglin AFB and sent to Vietnam for a trial deployment in late 1967. The concept was so successful that a formal RFP was put out in November 1967 and E-Systems of Dallas, Texas, was awarded a contract in December. By the end of the following year, four AC-130As, modified from JC-130As, were deployed to Vietnam, with three remaining behind for crew training until the following May when they too deployed to the combat zone. (Grant Matsuoka)

AC-130A, 55-0011, of the 711th SOS, 919th SOG, at Eglin AFB Field #3, July 1978. It is armed with a pair of 20mm M-61 and a pair of 40mm cannon. The eighth AC-130A incorporated several new systems, including a digital fire control computer. It was dubbed 'Surprise Package' and was so successful that the Air Force requested that the gunship systems program office provide an additional nine AC-130s in this configuration within three months. These were modified under the 'Pave Pronto' program. (N.E. Taylor)

M61 20mm Rotary Cannon

'Black Crow' AN/ASD-5 Direction Finding Radar

C-130A of the 109th TAS, 133rd TAW as photographed in February 1971 at Minneapolis. 55-0023 was among the first batch of C-130s delivered to the 463rd TCW in December 1956. It was later modified to NC-130A configuration and may have been a participant in clandestine operations, as evidenced by the black undersides. (C.B. Mayer)

(Below Left) 54-1633 was assigned to the 180th TAS, Missouri ANG when this picture was shot in August 1978. It is one of the early C-130As to receive four bladed props. (Fred Roos via N.E. Taylor)

The seventh C-130 built was still on active duty with the 433rd TAW, Kelly AFB, TX as of May 1976, when this picture was taken. (C. Eddy via Norm Taylor)

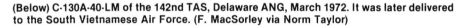

(Below) C-130A-40-LM of the 142nd TAS, Delaware ANG, March 1972. It was later delivered to the South Vietnamese Air Force. (F. MacSorley via Norm Taylor)

The first twelve C-130As for the Royal Australian Air Force were assigned USAF serial numbers from 57-498 through 57-509. The Austrialians coded them A97-3205 through -3216. (Lockheed via Norm Taylor)

C-130B

One of the things that has kept the C-130 going strong for over a quarter of a century is the constant improvement and adaptation of the basic design. The customers never seem to run out of new duties for the Herk, while Lockheed never seems to lack for innovative engineering to accomplish every mission tasked for the airplane. The first model change came in 1958, as the B model made its first flight on November 20.

The B model is generally considered to be the hotrod of the C-130 line. While it retained the lower payload of its predecessor, its engines were the more powerful 4,050shp T-56-A-7. The new four-bladed Hamilton-Standard props cut down on the noise level and vibration so pronounced in the earlier A models. The B also carried an additional 1820 gallons of fuel, giving it a longer range. In order to fully utilize this long range capability, crew bunks were installed which allowed for the carrying of a relief crew. The landing gear was also strengthened, as was the horizontal stabilizer. The former was in anticipation of the day when C-130s would be approved to carry higher gross weights, while the latter was a result of the ongoing test program, which had identified possible structural weaknesses in the stabilizer. A models were not retrofitted with the new stabilizers, but were limited to maximum speed of 287 knots.

As was the case with the A model, the B was adapted to many missions, which spawned several new prefixes to the basic identifier.

Curtiss-Electric Three-bladed Prop   Hamilton-Standard Four-bladed Prop

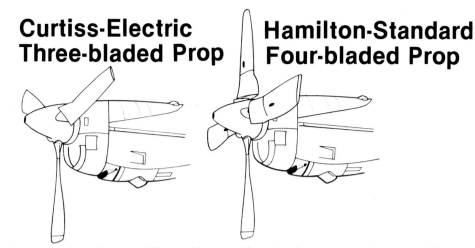

The second C-130B was modified to JC-130 configuration for use as an airborne satellite retriever. It is shown here during testing by the 6593rd Test Wing. (Note cameras under both wing tips and stabilizer.) (USAF via Norm Taylor)

(Left & Above) One of the vital humanitarian missions performed by the Hercules involves tracking and measuring the intensity of hurricanes. Lt. Gregory V. Wootton of the 53rd WRS is shown during the 1975 penetration of Hurricane Caroline. The WC-130B was the first of the Herks to be modified for hurricane hunting, entering service in 1962. The WC-130B illustrated above belonged to the 54th WRS, Keesler AFB, Miss., in October 1973. (Lockheed, D. Kasulka via Norm Taylor)

The National Oceanographic and Atmospheric Administration operated 58-0731 with civil registration N6541C in 1972. It was affectionately dubbed 'NOAA's Ark'. (MAP)

WC-130B Observation Blister

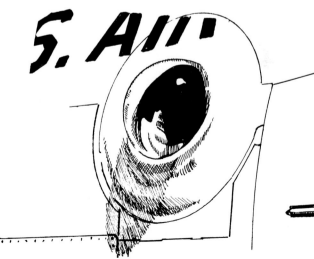

5. AII

C-130B of the 67th TAS, 433rd TAW, AFRES, Kelly AFB, Texas had tail camouflage modified to show its home state, October 1971. (Norm Taylor)

(Above Left) The office of this C-130B, 61-2647, seen at Offutt AFB, NE, 9 March 1980. (LTC George R. Cockle)

C-130B-70-LM of the Pakistan Air Force carried dark green camouflage. It was destroyed in July 1969. (via Norm Taylor)

(Below Left) 62-4141 was delivered to Pakistan under MAP, being operated by 6 Squadron of the PAF. Seen here at RAF Northolt in April 1965. (S. Peltz via Norm Taylor)

5-101 was the first C-130B-70-LM delivered to the Imperial Iranian Air Force. It was operated as a standard transport and was later sold to the Pakistan Air Force. (via Paul Stevens)

Canada operated four C-130Bs, three of which were eventually sold back to Lockheed. The fourth was destroyed in April 1966. (RCAF via Norm Taylor)

C-130B of the Venezuelan Air Force at Kelly AFB, Texas, December 1972. (Norm Taylor)

(Bottom Left) The three surviving RCAF C-130Bs were sold to Columbia. One is seen here at Howard AFB, Canal Zone, 1968. (Thomas J. Surlak via Dave Davenport)

South Africa acquired seven C-130Bs, all of which were operated by 28 Squadron, SAAF. (S. Peltz via Norm Taylor)

Nautical Herks

The natural intra-service rivalry between the Air Force and Navy usually results in a great deal of resistance if either service is put in the position of having to accept an airplane from the rival service. A notable exception to this almost irrefutable rule was the Navy adoption of the C-130.

Navy interest in the C-130 was sparked by the Marine Corps, which was looking for an assault transport that could double as an aerial refueller. The Air Force loaned the Navy a couple of C-130As, which went to Patuxent River NAS in 1957 for tests. The tests were predictably successful and the Marines placed their order for 46 KC-130Fs. They began taking delivery in 1960. 1960 was also the first year that the Herk went to the Poles on skis. Twelve C-130Ds of the 61st TCS, Sewart AFB, Tennessee, commanded by LtCdr. Wilbert Turk took on the job of trash hauling in the Antarctic. The job they did so impressed the Navy's Antarctic Station boss, Rear Admiral David M. Tyree, that the Navy had its own fleet of ski-equipped C-130s the following season. The C-130 has played the major resupply role in the Navy's operations at the Poles ever since, with first LC-130Fs eventually being supplanted by LC-130Rs.

Another maritime mission that the Herk seemed ideally suited for was the long range search role. The Coast Guard was quick to appreciate the attributes of the C-130B, which could be configured for search missions of up to 13 hours duration. They began taking delivery of their SC-130Bs (later redesignated HC-130B) in 1960.

But the most dramatic feat the Navy has asked of the Herk has to be landing on a carrier. These tests were conducted as a result of the Navy's realization that they needed a replacement for their range and payload limited C-1 Trader. The airplane they used was a KC-130F. The only modifications made were installation of an anti-skid braking system, smaller nose wheel orifice and removal of the wing-mounted refuelling pods. Pilot for the tests was Lt. James H. Flatley III, co-pilot was LtCdr. W.W. Stovall, engineer was ADR-1 E.F. Brennan and the safety pilot, who also checked Flatley out in the C-130 was Lockheed Engineering Test Pilot Ted Limmer, Jr. The tests were made on October 30, 1963. They included touch and gos, full stop unarrested landings and launches sans catapult. Weights were varied from a low of 85,000 lbs, to a high of 121,000 lbs. At the light weight, the KC-130F was stopped in just 270 feet and launched from that spot with the aid of 40 knots of relative wind over the deck. A total of 29 touch and gos and 21 full-stop landings and subsequent launches were made. The seas that day were relatively heavy, with swells up to 15 feet. Flatley's skill and airmanship that day earned him the DFC. The feasibility of using the C-130 for COD had been demonstrated, but the program went no further. Official reasons for dropping the idea were given as its being too risky. A more likely reason is that the 130 was just too big to be stored in the hangar or on the flight deck. This would necessitate mandatory round trips, which would inhibit carrier flexibility. In any case, the COD version of the E-2 was in the works and the Navy decided to wait for it.

The second KC-130F (BuNo 147573) for the Marines. (via Dave Davenport)

KC-130F of VMGR-352, MCAS El Toro, California refuels a pair of F-8 Crusaders in the early '60s. (USMC)

17

The U.S. Coast Guard has operated the C-130 since 1960, beginning with the HC-130B. (right, USCG) A variety of color schemes have been employed, ranging from the natural metal airplane at right, to the white birds below, all of which are trimmed in orange (FS 28915) and blue. The HC-130B below carries Coast Guard registration 1351. Its serial number is 62-3755, and it was delivered in February 1963. (LTV Electrosystems via C.B. Mayer) The HC-130H at bottom of page was delivered in May 1968 and is serialled 67-7184. It has the distinction of being the 1,000th Hercules built. (C.B. Mayer)

(Above) KC-130F BuNo 149798 touches down on deck of the carrier *Forrestal* CVA-59 with props already in full reverse. This technique allowed unarrested full stop landings of the Herk on the CVA. (Lockheed) (Below) KC-130F takes off from *Forrestal*. The wingtip of the Herk cleared the carrier's island by 15 feet. During these tests it carried the inscription; '*Look Ma, Ho Hook!*' on its starboard side. (Lockheed via Dave Davenport)

The Blue Angels acquired the C-130 as a support aircraft in 1970. The first of the *Fat Alberts*, as the Blue's Herks have been dubbed, was this KC-130F, BuNo 150690. It was operated by VMGR-252 out of Pensacola while assigned to the Blues. It later served with VMGR-352, in much more mundane markings, out of MCAS El Toro. (Lockheed via Dave Davenport)

VXE-6, home-based at NAS Point Mugu, California, deploys to Christchurch, New Zealand in October of each year to support the summer scientific operations of the National Science Foundation, which funds the Navy "Icebird" operations. The Antarctic provides the toughest environment for Hercules operations. It is one of the world's great deserts, receiving no more than 2 inches average annual precip, and operations are conducted off of ice up to 12,000 feet above sea level. The changing surface of the ice, often concealed from pilots by blowing snow, is a regular cause of damage to the LC-130Fs and Rs that the Navy has operated in the Antarctic since 1962. LC-130R of VXE-6 is seen offloading cargo on the Antarctic ice. Colors are light grey bottom, dark grey top and orange tail and wing tips. (Lockheed)

KC-130F Refuelling Pod

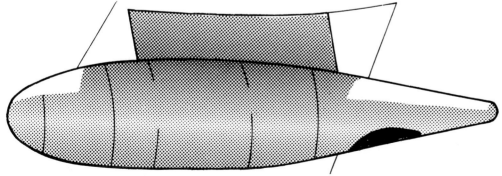

City of Christchurch, an LC-130F, came to grief in the Antarctic, burning at McMurdo in 1971. (Abbot Hafter via Paul Stevens)

19

DC-130A of Navy Squadron VC-3, based at NAS North Island, was originally a C-130A delivered to the USAF as 56-0491. Navy assigned BuNo 158229 to this drone launcher. The colors are grey and white with black fuselage band. The wings, horizontal tailplane and tail stripe are chrome yellow, the rest of the tail bright red.

Tacamo Antenna

EC-130Q of VQ-4, home-based at NAS Patuxent River, seen at RAF Mildenhall, 1972. The Navy refers to the EC-130 as 'Tacamo' and operates it as a manned communications relay link with the strategic submarine force. It can remain airborne for up to 13 hours and is designed as a survivable portion of the strategic communications network. The cone-shaped device under the rear fuselage is the main antenna. There are also extra wires running to the tail and a small whisker antenna at the tailtip. (P. Bennett via R. Archer)

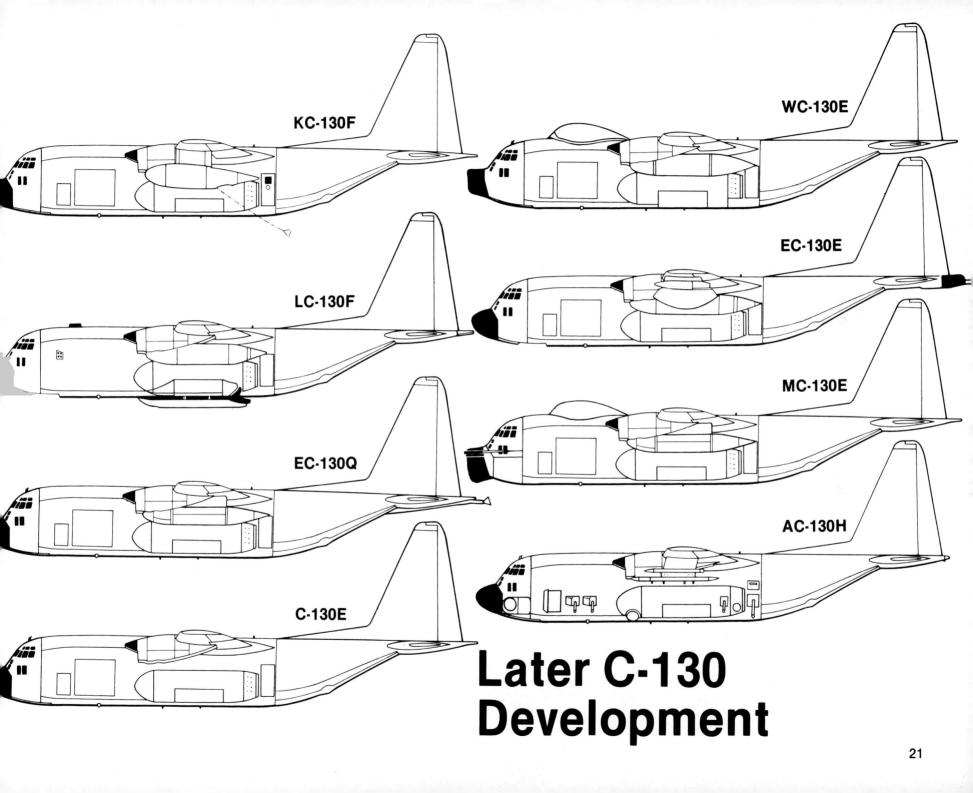

KC-130F

WC-130E

LC-130F

EC-130E

EC-130Q

MC-130E

C-130E

AC-130H

Later C-130
Development

C-130E

As it became more and more apparent that the vital interests of the United States were going to be placed in jeopardy by Communists the world over, the need for longer-ranged airlifters took on increased significance. The B model was the first of the beefed-up Hercules, but compared to what Lockheed's engineers did for the E, the B wasn't much different from the A.

Maximum ramp weight of the C-130E soared to 155,000 lbs., an increase of 20,000 lbs. over the 'B'. Its fuel capacity was increased by over 17,000 lbs. It was capable of non-stop flights to Europe with a 35,000 lb. payload and trans-Pacific flights could be made with one stop. All of this weight addition required extensive strengthening of the basic airframe, especially in the area of the wings and landing gear. More powerful T-56-A-7A engines of 4,050shp were used and a pair of external tanks with a capacity of 1360 gallons were slung beneath the wings, between the engines. The first C-130E was delivered to the Air Force on June 1, 1961. When the last of 488 C-130Es rolled off the the production line, it had more than doubled the combined production run for the 'A' and 'B' models. Only the 'H' model would be more numerous.

The first C-130E is rolled out of the plant. First flight took place on August 15, 1961, after it was delivered to the Air Force for testing on June 1, 1961. It was later modified to a JC-130E, then, later still, back to straight transport version. (USAF via Norm Taylor)

C-130E-90-LM of the 1501st ATW, Travis AFB at Elmendorf AFB, Alaska, May 1964. (Norm Taylor)

C-130E of the 314th Troop Carrier Wing at Forbes AFB, March 1966. This aircraft later destroyed when a prop went into reverse on take-off from Tainan AB, Taiwan in 1969. (Jerry Geer)

Airlift Pentagon at Pope AFB, NC in 1965 shows then operational USAF transport types including a venerable Dakota. (USAF via Davenport)

C-130E-95-LM of the 779th TAS, homebased at Pope AFB, NC on the transit line at Elmendorf AFB, Alaska, July 1968. (Norman E. Taylor)

C-130E of the 345th MAS, 374th MAW, Clark AB, Philippines at Misawa AB, Japan, October 1975. (Norman E. Taylor)

(Below Right) C-130E of the 313th TAW, Forbes AFB, Kansas during a September 1972 demonstration of rocket assisted take-off. (Fred Roos via Norm Taylor)

C-130E of the 778th TAS, 464th TAW, Pope AFB, NC during LAPES (Low Altitude Parachute Extraction System) delivery in March 1968. He is several feet too high, which is liable to cause the load to dip its leading edge, dig into the ground and roll itself up in a ball of junk. (USAF via Davenport)

Proof that the Herk can bite back if improper technique is used. C-130E 63-7801 was destroyed on landing at Pope AFB, June 1967. (Davenport)

SKE (APN-169A) Antenna

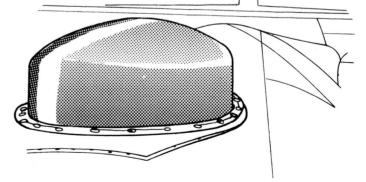

Front office of the C-130E, with SKE scope prominent atop panel. (Author)

C-130E in the desert camouflage that was applied to at least 30% of the Hercules fleet operated by USAF. Colors are tan and medium brown, low visibility national insignia and codes are also used. (R. Archer)

ABCCC Capsule (AN/USC-15)

(Airborne Battlefield Command & Control Center)

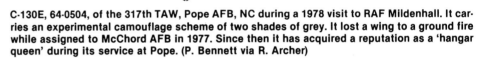

C-130E, 64-0504, of the 317th TAW, Pope AFB, NC during a 1978 visit to RAF Mildenhall. It carries an experimental camouflage scheme of two shades of grey. It lost a wing to a ground fire while assigned to McChord AFB in 1977. Since then it has acquired a reputation as a 'hangar queen' during its service at Pope. (P. Bennett via R. Archer)

(Below Left & Below) 62-1820 was the lead aircraft in the EC-130 program. Beginning in 1965, 10 aircraft were modified. They saw extensive duty in SEA, flying from Korat RTAB with the 388th TFW, where they carried 'JC' tail codes. Four were later further modified with dash 15 engines and inflight refuelling capability. (R.J. Wilmouth via Norm Taylor)

25

EC-130E Modifications

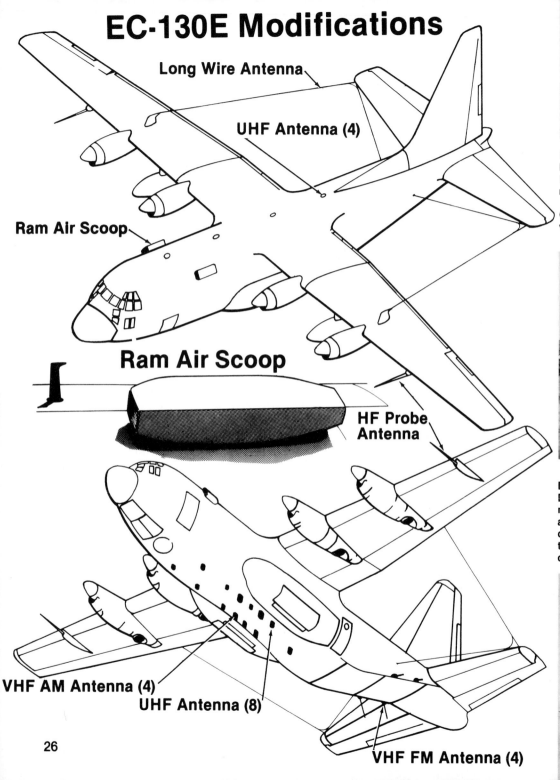

Long Wire Antenna

UHF Antenna (4)

Ram Air Scoop

Ram Air Scoop

HF Probe Antenna

VHF AM Antenna (4)

UHF Antenna (8)

VHF FM Antenna (4)

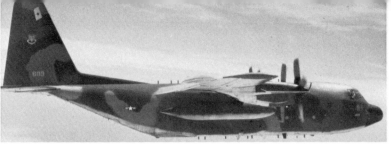

EC-130E, 62-1809, served with the 7th ACCS, 432nd TRW in combat in 1971, later converted to EC-130H and served with the 7th ACCS, 552nd ABEWG, Keesler AFB, Miss. It was lost in the Iranian Desert in the ill-fated attempt to rescue American Hostages, 25 April 1980. (Davenport Collection)

C-130E-II, 62-1820, while assigned 7th ACCS, 432nd TRW, Udorn RTAB. (USAF via Davenport)

EC-130E during refuelling from a tanker belonging to the Aeronautical Systems Division at Wright-Pat. EC-130 carries a crew of 4, plus 12 Battlestaff Crew manning the Capsule, which has 4 each HF Transceivers, VHF Transceivers and FM Transceivers, 8 UHF Transceivers, 2 secure Teletypewriters and 14 channels of Voice/Data Recorders. Its missions include management of tactical air resources, direct air support of ground forces and providing integrated communications. (R.J. Wilmouth via Norm Taylor)

MC-130E-110-LM, 64-0568, of the 8th SOS, 1st SOW, Hurlburt Field, Eglin AFB, FL. It carries the special low-reflectivity camouflage paint. (Norman E. Taylor)

MC-130E, of the 8th SOS, 1st SOW, began life as a C-130E, then received the dash one conversion (which later became the MC-130E) and, in 1978, the H (Combat Talon). Combat Talon Blackbirds have the Fulton Recovery System which allows in-flight recovery of personnel from the ground and Terrain Following Radar which allows all-weather operations to within 250 feet of the ground. (USAF via Davenport)

MC-130E of the 8th SOS refuelling from KC-97L, photographed by Captain Richard L. Bakke, who was KIA on the Iranian Hostage Rescue Mission, 25 April 1980. (via Grant Matsuoka)

Still another role for the ubiquitous Hercules is that of firefighter. The first MAFFS (Modular Airborne Fire Fighting System) tests were flown at Edwards AFB in 1971. More comprehensive tests were run in 1973 at Marana Air Park, Arizona, which resulted in acquistion by the U.S. Forest Service of several of the FMC Corp. MAFFS units. These are pre-positioned in anticipated 'hot' spots. If a fire warrants the use of the C-130, they can up-load the MAFFS pallets quickly and the mission can be flown with minimal additional workload to the basic crew. MAFFS units can be turned around in 10 minutes. They can dump up to 3,000 gallons of bright orange fire-retardant liquid nitrate compound in 10 seconds. The nitrate compound acts as a fertilizer when the fire has been extinguished. In these shots, C-130s of the 146th TAW, California ANG, (above) and 136th TAG, Texas ANG (right) are fighting a 1979 fire in the San Bernardino Mountains. (USAF) Both carry orange temporary markings. The California Herk is named *Ain't No Big Thing*.

An aerial delivery technique mastered by the Herk is LAPES. In the photo below, a record-setting 50,150 lb. load is pulled from the cargo hold. This heaviest of LAPES loads skidded to a halt after 700 feet. The test was conducted by the 6511th Test Group (Parachute) at El Centro, California. (Lockheed) In the photo at right, a Sheridan is about to arrive on the drop zone. (USAF)

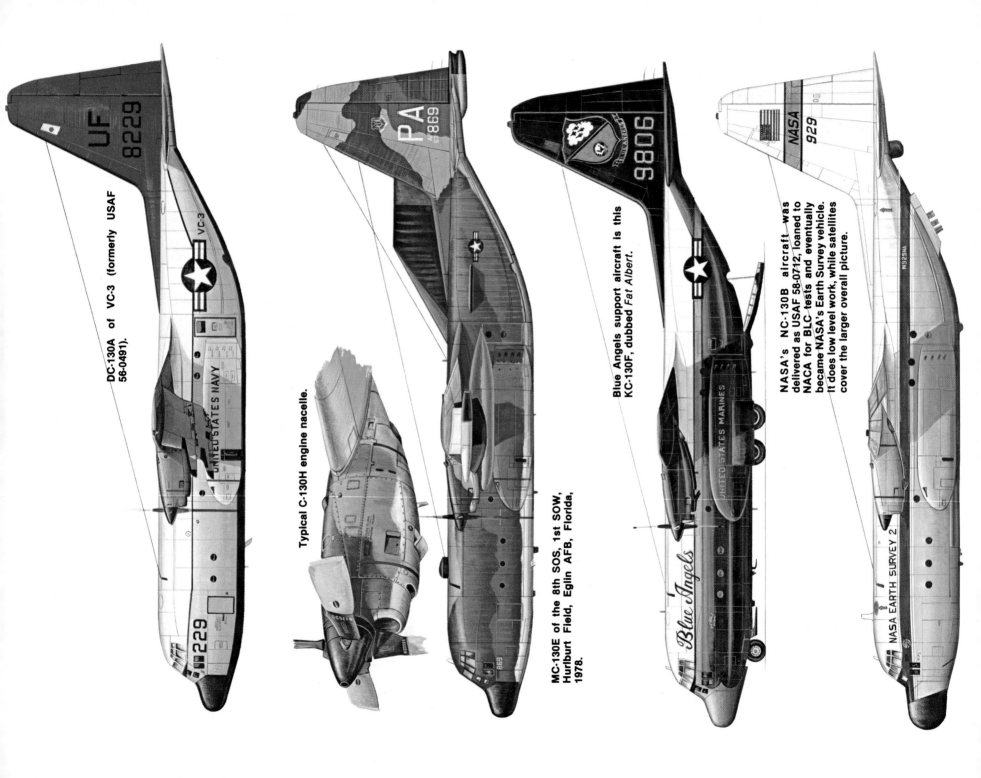

DC-130A of VC-3 (formerly USAF 56-0491).

Typical C-130H engine nacelle.

MC-130E of the 8th SOS, 1st SOW, Hurlburt Field, Eglin AFB, Florida, 1978.

Blue Angels support aircraft is this KC-130F, dubbed *Fat Albert*.

NASA's NC-130B aircraft was delivered as USAF 58-0712, loaned to NACA for BLC tests and eventually became NASA's Earth Survey vehicle. It does low level work, while satellites cover the larger overall picture.

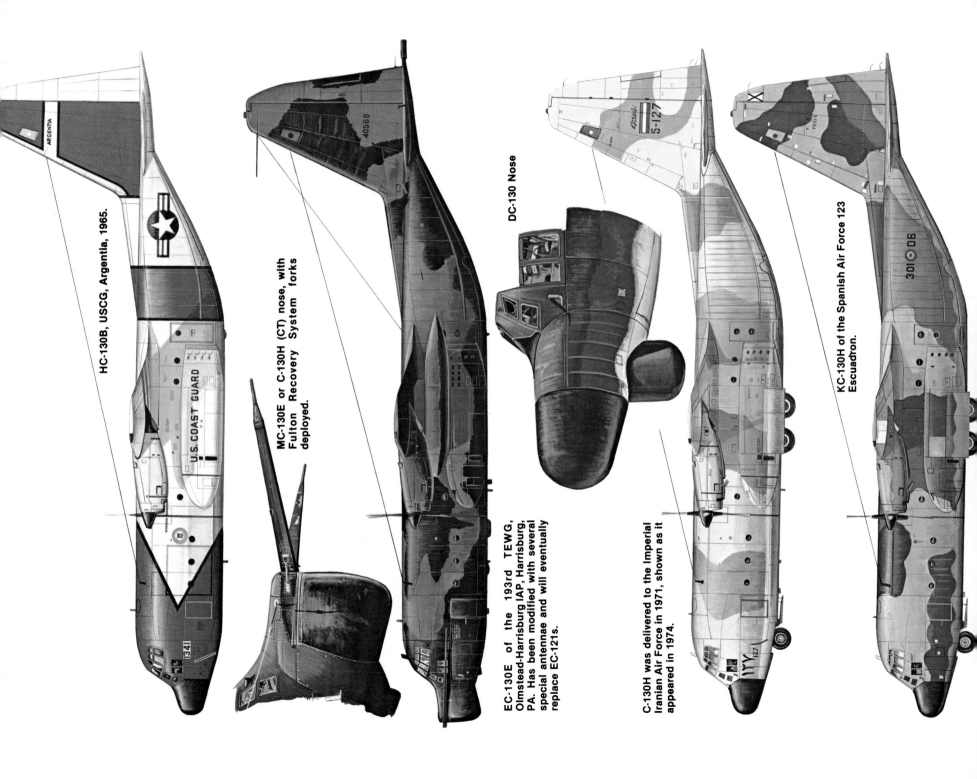

HC-130B, USCG, Argentia, 1965.

MC-130E or C-130H (CT) nose, with Fulton Recovery System forks deployed.

EC-130E of the 193rd TEWG, Olmstead-Harrisburg IAP, Harrisburg, PA. Has been modified with several special antennae and will eventually replace EC-121s.

DC-130 Nose

C-130H was delivered to the Imperial Iranian Air Force in 1971, shown as it appeared in 1974.

KC-130H of the Spanish Air Force 123 Escuadron.

AEP Pods

Lefthand Pod
(from below)

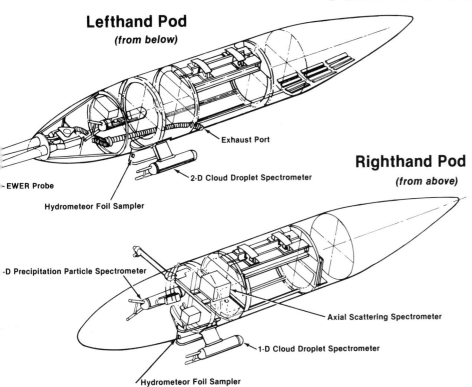

- EWER Probe
- Hydrometeor Foil Sampler
- Exhaust Port
- 2-D Cloud Droplet Spectrometer

Righthand Pod
(from above)

-D Precipitation Particle Spectrometer

- Axial Scattering Spectrometer
- 1-D Cloud Droplet Spectrometer
- Hydrometeor Foil Sampler

C-130E, 64-0571, was modified for the Aggravated Erosion Program. The modification consisted of adding special meteorological instrumentation, (most of which was contained in the two wing-mounted pods) and three operator stations, installed on pallets, in the fuselage cargo area. The right and left hand outer wings are of the HC-130H type which provide for hard points at the pod wing mounting locations. (LTC George R. Cockle, USA Ret.)

C-130E, A97-167 (USAF 65-12898), of No. 37 Squadron, Richmond RAAFB, Australia. (Lockheed via Davenport)

(Below Left) C-130E-105-LM was bought by the Swedish Air Force in 1965, then by the Swedish Red Cross who operated it in Biafra with civil registration SE-XBT until 1968. It was returned to the Air Force and camouflaged in 1975. (Capt. Humglot via Norm Taylor)

C-130E of the *Forca Aerea Brasileira* at Recife, Brazil, 1968. It was lost in December 1969. (Antonio Linhares via Davenport)

C-130E of 16 Squadron, Royal Saudi Air Force, at Kelly AFB, TX, October 1971. (Norman E. Taylor)

C-130E of the *Fuerza Aerea Argentina's* 2 Grupo de Transport, 1 Brigada Aerea, operated from El Palomar, Buenos Aires. TC-61 was the first Herk acquired by Argentina. (Reinhard via Taylor)

33

The C-130H

The H model of the Hercules is the penultimate version of the military 130s. As such, it had become the most produced of all 130 models, with orders for 565 as of the end of 1979. This latest rendition entered production in 1964 and has continued to benefit from advances in the state of the art. The H boasts increases of 26% in payload, 11% in speed, and 52% in range over the A model, while the takeoff distance requirement has been decreased by 17%.

These improvements have come as a result of the continuous efforts of Lockheed's engineering departments, coupled with Allison's improvement of the time-tested T-56 engine. The latest version of the T-56 for the Hercules is rated at 4,950 eshp for take-off, and 4,508 in flight. This allows a max take-off weight of 155,000 lbs. and a max cruise speed of 312.

In order to accommodate the greater weights allowed by the uprated engines, Lockheed has maintained an on-going structural improvements program. This program is responsible for the improved center wing box, which has increased the life span of the 130 while giving it the ruggedness necessary for higher payload missions. The new wing structure has been fatigue-tested to 40,000 simulated flight hours. At the current utilization rate, this will mean that you can plan on seeing 130s plying the airways of the world well into the 21st century. The new wing box has been retrofitted to all previous Air Force versions, with the exception of the A models, and to the 130s of Australia, New Zealand, Brazil, Iran, Pakistan, Saudi Arabia, Indonesia and Columbia.

The wing improvements did not stop with the center box, which was improved in 1969. In 1972 the outer wing panels were upgraded to the same fatigue standards. Over-all wing structural aluminum alloy has been upgraded to the new stress/corrosion resistant 7075-T73 material with the latest sulphuric acid anodized surface as a base for a newly developed polyurethane coating. In addition, wing box structures were fay-surface sealed on assembly with a corrosion-inhibitive polysulphide sealant. Structural fasteners were wet-installed with like material. External joints and seams are protected with environmental aerodynamic smoother/sealant. Added corrosion protection was given to the integral wing fuel tanks with the addition of a fuel boost pump-actuated water removal suction system, which had been pioneered in the design of the mammoth C-5A.

Perhaps the most dramatic improvements in the state of the art have come as a direct result of our manned space vehicles programs. The miniturization and enhanced reliability required for these programs have provided a cornucopia of technology for all aspects of modern life, but in no case has there been greater benefit than in the area of avionics.

The C-130 has provided a platform for all of these changes, spanning in its life the era of vacuum tube technology right through today's integrated circuits. The H models have the AN/APQ-122 (V)S Search and Weather Radar, dual 51V-4 Glide Slope Receivers, 51Z-4 Marker Beacon Receiver, AN/APN-171 Radar Altimeter, AN/APN-169A Intraformation Positioning Set, AN/ARN-97 Terminal Approach Landing Aid (Radar ILS), AN/APN-147 Doppler Navigator, ASN-35A Navigation Computer, the Air Force Standard Flight Director, the AN-URT-26 (V)8 Crash Position Locator and the Monitair Angle of Attack and Stall Warning System.

Other improvements incorporated in the latest 130s include a new auxiliary power unit, the model GTCP 85-180C. The new AiResearch APU is located in the landing gear pod, which has been extended forward 20 inches to accommodate it. The single package APU is flight operable to provide additional electrical power to the C-130. The flight controls system was improved with the addition of dual hydraulic systems driving tandem rudder control actuators, and aileron and rudder actuators have been improved through the use of new fatigue-resistant materials. The three hydraulic systems—utility, emergency and booster—were simplified and improved for greater reliability and better backup capability. The landing gear wheels are now made from forged aluminum for improved fatigue resistance, and the multi-disc brakes have a modulating individual wheel control anti-skid system for increased brake life and decreased fade during hard braking. The newest air conditioning system, developed for the S-3A Viking, has been likewise incorporated in current Herks.

The proof of the continuous improvement of the basic C-130 design has been its on-going popularity. Not only does it continue to add new customers to the Lockheed fold, but the old customers keep coming back for the newer versions. The Air Force has sponsored programs to develop replacements for the C-130, and two manufacturers have built and extensively tested prototypes for 130 replacements. In spite of this, they keep coming back to the 130. Its basic design has proven so adaptable to change that the per unit price just goes down (when adjusted for inflation). It is liable to be several years before someone comes up with the technology to finally render the remarkable Hercules obsolete. Until then, its domination of the world tactical air-lift scene is likely to remain absolute.

HC-130H-110-LM at Eglin AFB, Florida. First flight of the HC-130H was December 8, 1964. It entered service with MATS ARRS in 1965. (USAF via Norm Taylor)

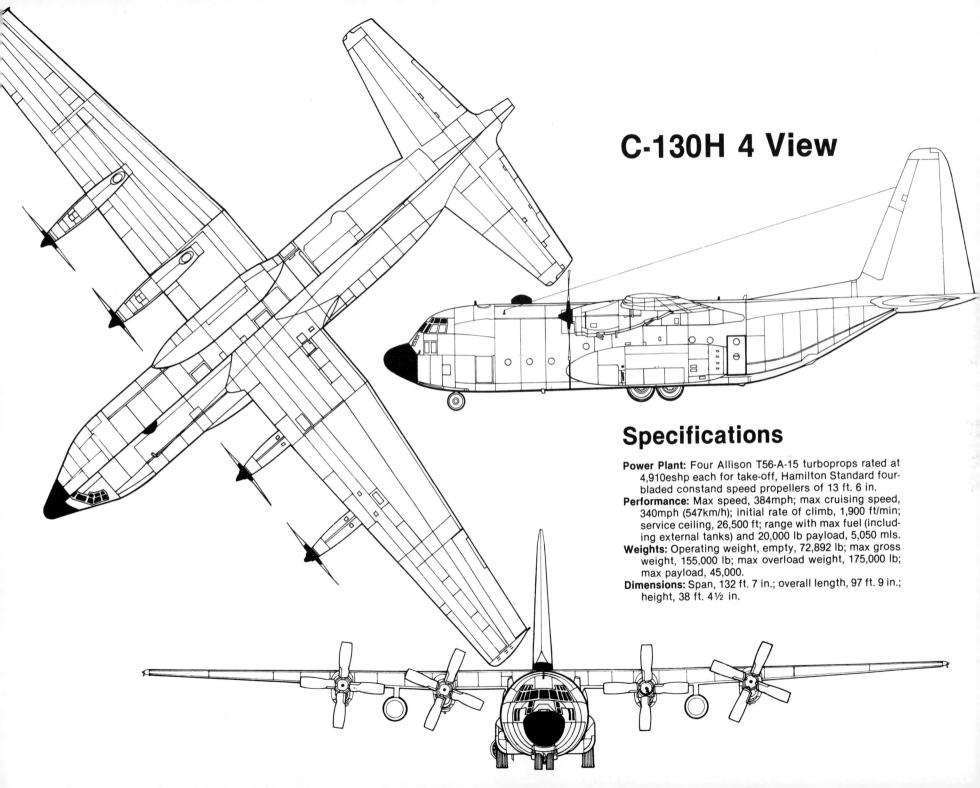

C-130H 4 View

Specifications

Power Plant: Four Allison T56-A-15 turboprops rated at 4,910eshp each for take-off, Hamilton Standard four-bladed constand speed propellers of 13 ft. 6 in.

Performance: Max speed, 384mph; max cruising speed, 340mph (547km/h); initial rate of climb, 1,900 ft/min; service ceiling, 26,500 ft; range with max fuel (including external tanks) and 20,000 lb payload, 5,050 mls.

Weights: Operating weight, empty, 72,892 lb; max gross weight, 155,000 lb; max overload weight, 175,000 lb; max payload, 45,000.

Dimensions: Span, 132 ft. 7 in.; overall length, 97 ft. 9 in.; height, 38 ft. 4½ in.

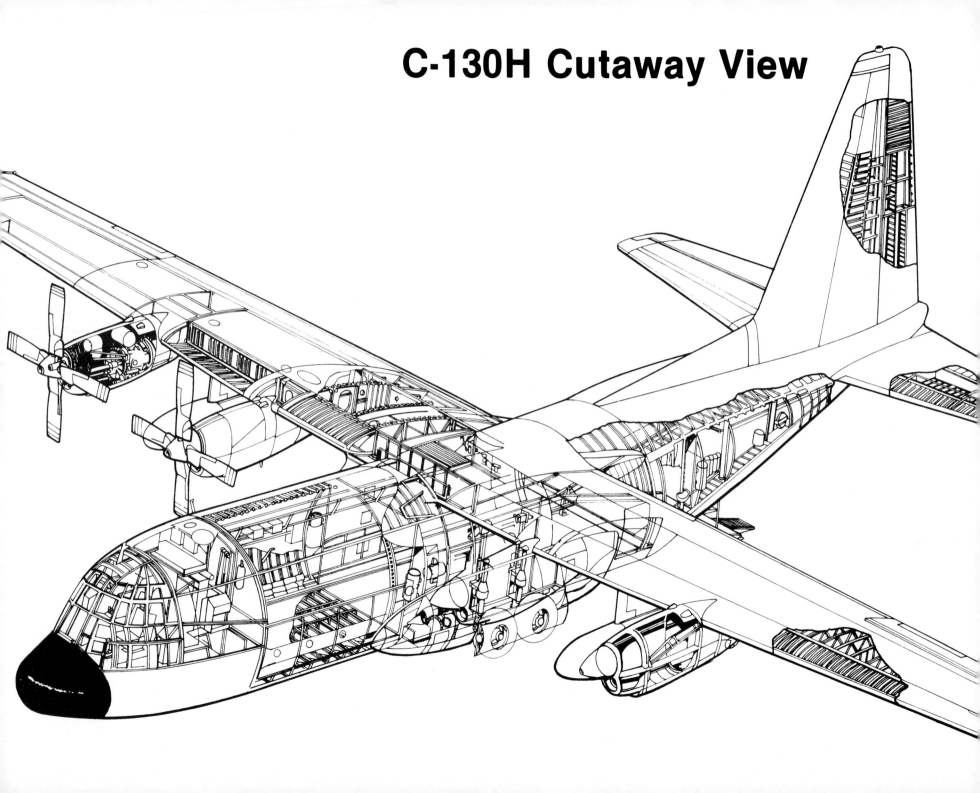

C-130H Cutaway View

HC-130H-120-LM of the 129th ARRS, Cal ANG, at Davis-Monthan AFB, July 1979. (B. Rogers, via Norm Taylor)

HC-130H with its 18 foot-long aluminum recovery forks deployed for a 'snatch' using the Fulton Recovery System. The system uses a helium balloon on the end of a 500 foot nylon line, with the 'snatchee' attached to the bottom end via harness. Herk will approach at 140 to 160mph, lock the line between the forks and reel in the load with a winch through the open rear cargo ramp. To prevent the line fouling the props, in the case of a miss, a pair of fiberglass lines run from the nose to the wingtips. The system has been proven in several live pickups, including a dual simultaneous snatch. (Lockheed)

C-130H (CT), 8th SOS, 1st SOW. Most informed speculation now has it that the Iran raiders used 3 C-130H (CT) Blackbirds and 3 EC-130Hs. The Blackbirds are configured and camouflaged for this type of mission, while the 3 ECs were 7th ACCS aircraft which had the capsules removed and fuel bladders installed for refuelling of the helicopters. The 7th ACCS aircraft are believed to be 62-1809, 62-1818, & 62-1857. They would have had their undersides painted flat black and low visibility markings applied. The Combat Talon Blackbirds carry AN/ALR-46 radar warning receivers, AN/AAQ-8 Infrared Countermeasures System, AN/ALE-27 Chaff Dispensers and FLIR (Forward Looking Infrared sensor). They navigate with an Inertial Navigation System, which can be updated with Loran and Doppler. (Norm Taylor)

HC-130N-165-LM of the 71st ARRS refuelling an HH-3 helicopter over Alaska, February 1978. (USAF AAC via Norm Taylor)

HC-130P-130-LM of the 129th ARRS, California ANG, Hayward ANGB, Cal., March 1977. (B. Rogers via Taylor)

HC-130N-165-LM landing at Kadena AB, Okinawa. Coincidental with its acquistion of the HC-130, the ARRS also received its first helicopters, the HH-3C. It immediately set about the task of providing an aerial refuelling capability for the helicopters, with the HC-130 as the tanker. Original intention was to give the helicopters world-wide range (this was successfully demonstrated with a non-stop flight from the East Coast to Paris), with a prime objective being recovery of astronauts. The HC-130N was the initial tanker version. Its capacity was similar to the KC-130F. The HC-130P has more powerful engines and additional tanker capacity with fuselage tanks added. (S. Ohtaki via Taylor)

AC-130H of the 4950th Test Wing, Aeronautical Systems Division, Wright-Patterson AFB, February 1977. 69-6577 began life as a C-130E, was modified to AC-130E and then to AC-130H in 1973. (R.J. Mills, Jr.)

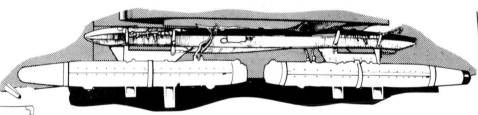

AN/ALQ-87 ECM Pods

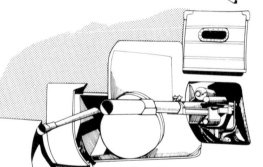

M2A1 40mm gun, AN/APQ-150 Beacon Tracking Radar & 105mm gun

Forward Crew Entry Door

AN/AJQ-24 Stabilized Tracking Set, AN/ASQ-145 Low Light Television and AN/AVQ-19 Laser Target Designator/Ranger

The follow-on program to Pave Pronto gunships was the Pave Spectre modification program begun in 1972. Under Pave Spectre and Pave Spectre II (AC-130E and H respectively), the Hercules was given greatly increased firepower, sensing equipment and defensive devices. AC-130H-160-LM of the 16th SOS, 1st SOW, Hurlburt Field, Eglin AFB, Florida, March 1980. Rare look at the starboard side of a gunship shows the scanner/observer position above forward portion of wheel well fairing. (Norman E. Taylor)

(Above Right) One of a pair of M61A1 20mm guns carried by the AC-130. (R.J. Mills, Jr.)

Forward fuselage of AC-130H, 69-6572, which was delivered in August 1969 as a C-130E, later modified to AC-130E and then upgraded to AC-130H in 1973. AN/ASD-5 Black Crow Direction Finding Set is carried on port side of fuselage under cockpit. (R.J. Mills, Jr.)

Pave Spectre II (AC-130H)

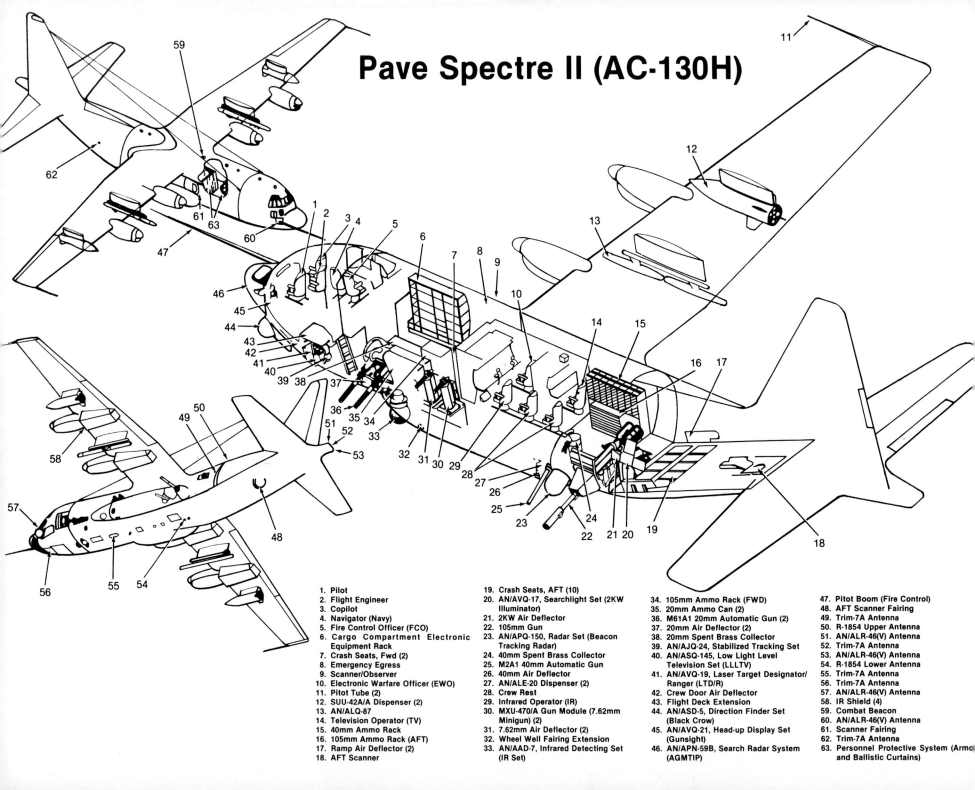

1. Pilot
2. Flight Engineer
3. Copilot
4. Navigator (Navy)
5. Fire Control Officer (FCO)
6. Cargo Compartment Electronic Equipment Rack
7. Crash Seats, Fwd (2)
8. Emergency Egress
9. Scanner/Observer
10. Electronic Warfare Officer (EWO)
11. Pitot Tube (2)
12. SUU-42A/A Dispenser (2)
13. AN/ALQ-87
14. Television Operator (TV)
15. 40mm Ammo Rack
16. 105mm Ammo Rack (AFT)
17. Ramp Air Deflector (2)
18. AFT Scanner

19. Crash Seats, AFT (10)
20. AN/AVQ-17, Searchlight Set (2KW Illuminator)
21. 2KW Air Deflector
22. 105mm Gun
23. AN/APQ-150, Radar Set (Beacon Tracking Radar)
24. 40mm Spent Brass Collector
25. M2A1 40mm Automatic Gun
26. 40mm Air Deflector
27. AN/ALE-20 Dispenser (2)
28. Crew Rest
29. Infrared Operator (IR)
30. MXU-470/A Gun Module (7.62mm Minigun) (2)
31. 7.62mm Air Deflector (2)
32. Wheel Well Fairing Extension
33. AN/AAD-7, Infrared Detecting Set (IR Set)

34. 105mm Ammo Rack (FWD)
35. 20mm Ammo Can (2)
36. M61A1 20mm Automatic Gun (2)
37. 20mm Air Deflector (2)
38. 20mm Spent Brass Collector
39. AN/AJQ-24, Stabilized Tracking Set
40. AN/ASQ-145, Low Light Level Television Set (LLLTV)
41. AN/AVQ-19, Laser Target Designator/ Ranger (LTD/R)
42. Crew Door Air Deflector
43. Flight Deck Extension
44. AN/ASD-5, Direction Finder Set (Black Crow)
45. AN/AVQ-21, Head-up Display Set (Gunsight)
46. AN/APN-59B, Search Radar System (AGMTIP)

47. Pitot Boom (Fire Control)
48. AFT Scanner Fairing
49. Trim-7A Antenna
50. R-1854 Upper Antenna
51. AN/ALR-46(V) Antenna
52. Trim-7A Antenna
53. AN/ALR-46(V) Antenna
54. R-1854 Lower Antenna
55. Trim-7A Antenna
56. AN/ALR-46(V) Antenna
57. AN/ALR-46(V) Antenna
58. IR Shield (4)
59. Combat Beacon
60. AN/ALR-46(V) Antenna
61. Scanner Fairing
62. Trim-7A Antenna
63. Personnel Protective System (Armor and Ballistic Curtains)

Hercules W2 of the Meteorological Research Flight, RAE Farnborough, landing at RAF Mildenhall, 1977. The former RAF C-130K has been extensively modified for its current mission. Mods include 22 foot long nose probe, which necessitated moving the radar antenna to a pod atop the fuselage. (P. Bennett via R. Archer)

(Above Right) The C-130Hs of No. 40 Squadron, Royal New Zealand Air Force, Whenuapai RNZAFB, Auckland City, N.Z. in July 1969. (RNZAF via Davenport)

(Below) The C-130Hs of the 20th Wing, Royal Belgian Air Force carry the basic USAF camouflage colors and patterns. Note Loran antenna atop rear fuselage, Paris, June 1977. (F. Humblot via Norm Taylor)

(Above) Portuguese Air Force C-130H. Portugal has five Herks, all finished in basic USAF camouflage. (H. Scharringa via Norm Taylor)

(Left) Royal Hellenic Air Force C-130H at Mildenhall, 1978. This is a late model 'H' delivered in 1977 in USAF colors. (P. Bennett via R. Archer)

43

Denmark's 721 Squadron operates 3 C-130Hs in dark green camouflage with dayglo nose, fuselage and wingtip bands. The Hercules has had a profound effect on the economic life of all of the free world, providing a desperately needed boost to US balance of payments and giving underdeveloped countries the means to hasten development of their own resources. Though the majority of the Hercules fleet worldwide carries warpaint of one variety or another, most of the missions performed by that fleet are far more humanitarian in nature than those of any other aircraft flying today, commercial or military. (Lockheed via Davenport)

C-130K of No. 35 Squadron RAF at Paris, June 1977, in recent RAF camouflage scheme of green and grey. (F. Humblot via Norm Taylor)

(Above Left) C-130H of the Abu-Dhabi Air Force carries an unusual camouflage scheme of sand and dark green. This is the second half of Abu-Dhabi's C-130 fleet. (Lockheed)

C-130H of the Egyptian Air Force carries civil registration for international flights. It is in camouflage scheme peculiar to Egyptian and Morrocan 130s of cream and tan overall. (C. Eddy via Norm Taylor)

C-130K of RAF in earlier camouflage of dark earth and mid-stone with black undersurfaces (MOD via Davenport)

C-130H for Bolivia's *Transporte Aereo Militar*. The first of two C-130Hs for Bolivia. (Lockheed via Davenport)

(Above, Left, Below Left) Israel has operated the C-130 for several years, the first of the ID-FAF Hercules coming directly from USAF inventory. (Note USAF camouflage on Israeli 130 at left at Ben Gurion Airport, Tel-Aviv.) Most Israeli 130s are finished in desert camouflage and carry civil registration. In one of the most acclaimed rescue missions in history, the Israeli Air Force flew a force of IDF commandos over 2400 miles to Entebbe, Uganda to rescue hostages that were being held after the hijacking of an Air France flight from Tel-Aviv. *Operation Thunderball* on July 4, 1976 was one of the Herk's finest hours. (P. Bennett via R. Archer, R. Archer via Davenport and via Davenport.)

(Below) C-130H-115-LM of the Royal New Zealand Air Force at the International Air Tattoo, June 23-24, 1979, RAF Greenham Common, England. Twenty-seven Herks from 15 different countries showed up to celebrate the silver anniversary of the C-130. In spite of the fact that this 130, delivered in 1964, had over 10,000 hours on its airframe, it was still adjudged the cleanest Herk in attendance and was awarded the *Concours d'Elegance* trophy. Colors are white, gloss gray and blue trim. (H. Scharringa via Norm Taylor)

Combat

Far from being just the penultimate 'trash hauler' of the entire war zone, the Hercules may have been the most versatile aircraft in the war in Southeast Asia. Not only did it pioneer aerial delivery techniques that ranged from ground level (LAPES) to over 10,000 feet (AWADS), it acted as troop transport, paratroop platform, ambulance, command and control platform, gunship, drone launcher, tanker, rescue and recovery vehicle, weather recce and, finally, when it was time to go into Hanoi to bring the POWs home, the Herk was the first aircraft to land at Gia Lam.

The LAPES method of delivery is covered elsewhere in this book. AWADS was instituted during the Spring 1972 NVA offensive, when AA in South Vietnam increased to a level of intensity that forced the relatively vulnerable C-130s to altitudes above 10,000 feet. Using onboard radar and computers, the navigator would use offset aiming points to release the load. Special cushioning on the pallets allowed use of high speed parachutes, which helped negate the vagaries of unreported low altitude winds. These loads smacked into the drop zone at better than 60 mph. They were 90% accurate, with most misses occurring as a result of parachute malfunctions.

Another largely unreported C-130 activity concerned the rainmaking efforts of specially modified WC-130s operating from Udorn AB, Thailand from 1967 through mid-1972. Silver iodide flares were dropped into likely looking clouds with mixed results. This in an effort to impede the flow of supplies down the Trail.

The Hercules was also used as a bomber, dropping 15,000 pound bombs during the South Vietnamese invasion of Laos. These blockbusters were dropped on suspected troop concentrations and had the residual effect of creating instant helicopter landing zones. The USAF lost 53 C-130s during their participation in the Vietnam War. Many of the survivors were turned over to the RVNAF and one of these set an all-time record for passengers on its last flight from Tan Son Nhut AB, April 29, 1975. The C-130A was loaded with 452 people, including 32 in the cockpit! It took over 10,000 feet of runway to become airborne and landed at Utapao, Thailand 3½ hours later. This brilliant piece of airmanship was performed by RVNAF IP Major Phuong and he did it without benefit of a co-pilot! A truly herculean effort by both airplane and pilot!

C-130B from 772nd TAS, 463rd TAW at Phu Cat AB, RVN, February 1971. (Norm Taylor)

Another squadron from the 463rd, the 773rd, supported the Marines at Khe Sanh in 1968. Marines referred to the big transports as 'mortar magnets'.

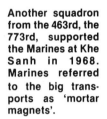

Beleaguered garrison at Khe Sanh depended solely upon airlift for resupply. (USAF via Taylor)

C-130B, 58-754, of the 774th TAS' 463rd TAW, out of Clark AB, Philippines, during conveyer deployment to Vietnam in 1968. Typical combat airstrip Herk operated into and out of throughout the war. (USAF via Davenport)

HC-130P refuels HH-3E off the Vietnamese coast, 1969. This team played the major role in rescue of downed airmen in SEA war. (USAF via Taylor)

HC-130N at Takhli, 1970. (Col. Don Kutyna)

C-130E 64-0515 'Greybirds' from E Flight were the aircraft used for clandestine operations into Laos, Cambodia and Points North. Note that the national insignia is close by the paratroop door, where it can be easily covered. (Dave Davenport)

C-130Es of the 345th TAS, 314th TAW, out of Ching Chuan Kang ROCAB, at Firebase North, Danang, RVN in August 1970. A graphic example of the reliance on the C-130 for combat airlift and of the weather the 130 operated in during the Vietnam War. (Davenport Collection.)

C-130B, 58-0743, came to grief at Tan Son Nhut AB during the Tet Offensive of 1968. (Davenport Collection)

AC-130A of the 16th SOS gets an engine change at Ubon, June 1969. (USAF)

"HAVE A NICE WAR"

C-130 ABCCC aircraft were the airborne command posts of the air war in Southeast Asia. They carried call signs such as *Alleycat, Moonbeam, Cricket* and *Hillsboro*, and directed the ebb and flow of aerial forces. (USAF)

AC-130A of the 16th SOS, 8th TFW at Ubon, RTAB, 1970. *The Exterminator* was applied in red and white. It was 54-1628 and was coded FT. (Davenport Collection)

AC-130A, 56-509, of the 16th SOS, 8th TFW over Laos in 1972. Standard USAF camouflage on top surfaces, with black bottom and vertical surfaces. 'FT' and serial in red. (Davenport Collection)

16th SOS AC-130 climbs out over the steaming jungles of Thailand during the 1972 SEA fighting. (USAF)

Details of initial installation of the 20mm vulcan cannon in the first AC-130A. Also visible are the 7.62mm miniguns. (USAF via Norm Taylor)

AC-130A of the 16th SOS, 8th TFW at Ubon, RTAFB, Thailand, April 1969. Standard USAF camouflage carried on upper surfaces, flat black under and on vertical surfaces. Red codes on tail. (Al Piccirillo via Norm Taylor)

AC-130A, 54-1626, at Ubon RTAFB, 1968. Devastating effectiveness of gunships was demonstrated in *Operation Commando Hunt*, which was the attempt to destroy supplies marshalled in North Vietnam with impunity under the protection of LBJ's bombing halt of 1968. *Commando Hunt* took place along the Laotian Ho Chi Minh trail. It destroyed an estimated 66% of all supplies put into the pipeline. Gunships accounted for about half of this. (Norm Taylor Collection)

(Below) During the oil exploration boom on the north slope of Alaska, the rugged dependability of the Hercules made it the premier airlifter for the oil fields. This L-100 was operated by Interior Airlines from Anchorage, July 1972. (Norman E. Taylor)

(Above) L-100, N9263R, Alaska Airlines, Anchorage, Alaska, 1966. Four different airlines have owned this Herk. (Lockheed via Davenport)

The Commercial Hercules

The most successful transport aircraft in history, the DC-3/C-47 achieved much of its popularity and longevity through military production and civilian utilization. Mindful of the lessons in this, the engineers at Lockheed decided to submit the C-130 for civil certification in the mid-'sixties. This would ensure continued use of retired military aircraft and might possibly open new markets for sales of a civilian version of the C-130.

The first civil version of the Hercules, the Model 382 L-100 was subsidized in large measure by the sub-contractors of the C-130 systems, who donated their products to build a company demonstrator aircraft. Its first flight was on April 20, 1964. It was later modified to an L-100-20 and flew with a number of airlines before being sold to the Philippine Government. Lockheed sold 21 L-100s, 25 L-100-20s and has to date sold 30 L-100-30s, which makes it an unqualified commercial success. With every stretch, the Hercules becomes more competitive, since its cost per ton-mile has begun to better that of small and medium size pure jets. The future of the Commercial Herk may be in the dash 50 model proposed by Lockheed in 1979. Modifications include 501-D22E engines, a new landing gear fairing (similar to those on the C-141), and insertion of a 20 foot plug in the forward fuselage and a 16 foot plug in the rear fuselage, which would put overall length at 133 feet. The dash 50 is aimed at regional cargo transport operators that need wide-body capacity to interconnect with smaller airports.

Another possiblity for the future is the model 400, a twin engine variant of the C-130. It would retain the basic L-100 fuselage, and use the Allison 502-D22D turboprop engines on a shorter wing. Development of the model L-400 was given the go-ahead in early 1980. The first is expected to begin flying in 1982. Commonality of these follow-on versions to earlier models of the C-130/L-100 series should ensure use of the Hercules in commercial ventures well into the next century.

L-100-20 stretched version of the commercial Herk operated by Red Dodge Aviation on lease from Flying W Airways, Anchorage, May 1969. (Norman E. Taylor)

Commercial Hercules Development

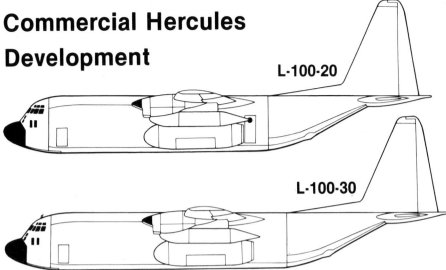

L-100-20

L-100-30

L-100-20 of Southern Air Transport, one of the airlines organized under the aegis of the CIA. At Miami IAP, August 1970. (Lockheed via Davenport)

This pair of L-100-20s was originally sold to Flying W Airways in 1970, returned to Lockheed and refurbished and sold to Peru in 1973. (Lockheed via Davenport)

Saturn Airlines prevailed upon Lockheed to further stretch the Herk when it won a contract to ferry Rolls Royce Engines from England to Palmdale for installation in the Lockheed TriStar. Deletion of the Paratroop Doors and ATO attachment points allowed a stretch of 6'8½" without a great increase in empty weight. With this stretch, Saturn was able to carry a full set of three of the RR RB-211 Engines. This was given designation L-100-30. *Rudolph* was photographed at Kelly AFB, Texas, December 1971. (Norm Taylor)

These L-100s are two of those flown by the airforce of Gabon. The -20 below and the -30 above carry identical color schemes (white and aluminum with blue stripe) but quite different markings. L-100-20 was delivered to the Forces Aeriennes Gabonaises (Gabon Air Force) in December 1976. Seen at Paris, June 1977. (F. Humblot via Taylor, Lockheed)

Future Herks

Early in 1972, the USAF requested proposals from industry on an Advanced Medium STOL Transport. The two finalists in the AMST sweepstakes were the Boeing YC-14 and the McDonnell Douglas YC-15. Both reflected state-of-the-art approaches to the problem of hauling troops and their equipment intra-theater. Both were tested extensively in prototype configuration and, though they promised reliability and inhanced capability through technological advancement, they lacked the clout necessary to assure continued funding, which ran out in FY 1979.

Following the settling of the Boeing and McDonnell Douglas AMSTs into the obscurity of non-funding, Lockheed-Georgia proposed two 'low cost' derivatives of the C-130 for the role. Testifying before Congress, Lt. Gen. Tom Stafford, Air Force deputy chief of staff for research, development and acquisition stated that "in the absence of continued funding of AMST, the Air Force might be forced to rely upon modified versions of the C-130 to fill its airlift needs into the '80s". The two advanced versions of the Herk proposed included an improved volume loadability speed (VLS) version, and a Wide Body STOL (WBS) version. The primary reason for this concern for a new airplane was caused by the larger size of air-transportable Army combat equipment.

The WBS version would have its fuselage enlarged in height from 9.1 feet to 11.3 feet, in width from 10 to 11.7 feet and in length from 41.4 to 48.1 feet. The wings and engine support structures would be strengthened to accomodate T-56-A-15 engines with a new 14 foot diameter prop. It would have floor and loading ramp strengthened to allow for the heavier loads, roll control spoilers and the single-piece Fowler flaps would be replaced with double-slotted flaps. It also would have stronger landing gear, which would allow heavier gross landing weights and higher sink rates. Additional directional control would be available through a larger chord rudder and dorsal fin. It would be air-refuellable and would meet all of the requirements established for the AMST by the Air Force.

The second advanced C-130 concept proposed by Lockheed was the so-called VLS, which incorporates the following features; the aft cargo loading door increased in size, drag reduced by the addition of a T-tail which, in conjunction with Allison DDA 501-M-71 engines of 5,600 eshp driving 14 foot diameter props, would raise the cruise speed to 360 knots at 20,000 feet, fuel economy increased by 21% in high speed cruise and 9% in long range cruise and interior volume and unrefueled range both increased by 33%. Lockheed estimated development costs of about 500 million dollars for either version, a mere pittance in the 1980's world of mega-million dollar defense contracts.

Efforts to develop new versions of the Herk were not limited to larger, more complex derivatives. In January 1980, Lockheed-Georgia was given a go-ahead by the parent company to develop a twin engine version of the C-130. The twin Herk is aimed at the export market, with a projected price tag of about 70 to 80% of that of the L-100. The twin engine

C-130 has been designated L-400 and is to begin flying in the spring of 1982, with first deliveries slated for early in 1983. The L-400 would use the standard L-100 fuselage with 22 feet less wing span, but will have Allison 501-D22F engines of 4,900 shaft horsepower driving 14 foot diameter props and be equipped with a water-alcohol injection system to permit the higher take-off thrust required at high density altitudes. Max gross weight of the L-400 was projected at 84,000 lbs.

Back again in the opposite direction, Lockheed has proposed a replacement for the EC-130Q TACAMO aircraft in April 1980. The proposal to the U.S. Navy envisioned the most ambitious stretch of the basic design to date. It would be powered by three General Electric/Snecma CFM-56 jet engines, have a larger fuselage, super-critical wing and a gross take-off weight of 250,000 lbs, which would give it a 60% increase in payload!

Three artist's conceptions of proposed C-130 derivatives. (Above) The WBS, (Below) the VLS and (Below Left) the L-400.

Epilog

1 May 1980—407th Supply and Service Battalion, 82nd Airborne Division— Drop Zone Salerno, Fort Bragg, N.C.—Parachute Type MC-1—Type Jump, Combat Equipment—Type Aircraft, C-130—Remarks: "You can't go home again."

Early in the preparation of this book, I decided that I would like to return to the scene of my introduction to the C-130, and to go along on a troop drop mission. I wanted to see if things were as I remembered them. They weren't.

My first clue that time had not stood still for twenty-four years came upon arrival at the Fayetteville airport. Gone was the quaint old terminal building that seemed to fit so well the DC-3-equipped Piedmont Airlines of 1956. In its place was a modernistic shell more in keeping with the 1980s B-737 equipped Piedmont. A four-lane expressway, appropriately christened the 'All American Freeway', now stretched from Fayetteville to the Fort Bragg-Pope AFB complex. So far, no rush of nostalgia and I went to bed that night fearing that everything would have been changed....that all my links to the past....those brief, but important years spent here....would have disappeared without a trace.

Things began to look a little more familiar when I arrived at the troop marshalling area the next morning. A few buildings remained from my time, including the large building that had been used to pack parachutes. It was now the headquarters of the 82nd Airborne Division Jumpmaster School, which was in session. I was comforted to see that the 82nd still knew the value of highly starched fatigue uniforms and spit-shined boots. But the C-46 and C-119 mockups were gone, as were the old wooden PLF platforms. In their places were several C-130 mockups and concrete platforms....and these looked like they had been around for several years.

Looking out at the ramp, I could see that other changes had been made. One of the runways had disappeared, completely paved over to provide additional parking space. In the days when C-119s and C-123s were assigned to Pope, there had been two long perpendicular runways with adjacent parking areas of grass. It may not have been a perfectly sylvan setting, but I always thought that there was something great about being able to sprawl in the grass after you got 'chuted up, while you were waiting to board the airplane. The grass seemed to add a barnstorming flavor to each jump and, as anyone who has ever resented the regimen of military life will tell you, opportunities to feel freedom within that life are to be savored and remembered fondly. The grass was gone, replaced with concrete. Prelude to additional shocks.

As we approached the troops of the 82nd Airborne who would be making the jump, and were just arriving in the marshalling area, my Air Force escort said, incredulously; "I think I see a girl!" He did. In fact, there were several women in this planeload of 52 jumpers and compounding the surprise was the revelation that the jumpmaster was a woman....a not unattractive woman, I might add. She was Captain Vallie J. Pratt. The competent manner in which she put the troops through their mockup drill left no doubt who was in charge.

The official position on women in the Army is that they won't be assigned to combat units. But there is a fine line between what is officially a 'combat unit', and a 'combat-related unit', and the Army is less conservative on this issue than most people might imagine. Even before women's rights became a *cause celebre*, the Army was quietly guaranteeing equal opportunities for women. Job assignments are determined by merit, not by sex. This policy has led to women in the role of instructors, administrators, mechanics, communications specialists, medical technicians, pilots, military police and (**gulp**) paratroopers. They have been assigned to the 82nd Airborne Division since 1978. I admit it....I am not liberal enough to completely escape the taint of male chauvinism and I had imagined that occupations such as paratrooper might still remain bastions of macho. Not so, and the attitudes of the male troopers didn't seem to indicate any deference to the females, with the possible exception that there seemed to be a lack of some of the more common colloquialisms.

Suffering slightly from future shock, I decided to walk out to the airplane and see if it had changed as much as its passengers. This airplane had been around. It was a C-130E, serial number 63-7792. It had been delivered to Military Airlift Command on November 5, 1963, and had served at Dyess AFB, Texas and Langley AFB, Virginia prior to its current

duty with the 36th TAS, 62nd Military Airlift Wing at McChord AFB, Washington. It had brought its crew TDY to Pope for training. It sported a fairly recent application of the three-tone USAF camouflage, complete with the new, low visibility markings which belied its age. It had been well maintained on the inside, too, and I doubt that anyone would have guessed its true age.

Ours was to be the lead ship in a two-plane formation. Number two in the formation would be two to four thousand feet in trail and would keep that distance with the aid of SKE (Station Keeping Equipment), now carried on most MAC C-130s. SKE displays the relative position of the other aircraft in the formation on a radar scope mounted atop the panel between the pilots. Captain Bob Polakoski was getting checked out as a formation leader and he would be flying the left seat, while the aircraft commander, Captain Harry Holliday, checked him out from the right seat. Navigator was Lt. Tim O'Hagan, Engineer was Sgt. James Jones and the loadmasters were Sgts. Ron Smith and Ron Johnson. We were briefed for a 40 minute flight to the DZ. After takeoff we would cancel IFR and fly a low-level VFR route to the drop zone. This was in keeping with combat conditions, with the troop carriers coming in low (500 feet) and fast in an attempt to evade radar detection. In combat, the troops would probably be dropped from 500 feet, or lower, to minimize their exposure to hostile fire. Today we would be dropping them from 1250 AGL.

As I strapped myself in on the crew bunk immediately behind the engineer, the pilots were completing their pre-start checklist. Starting the C-130 is straightforward and simple. With the throttles in the ground idle position, the power levers are moved from Stop to Run and the start button is held in until RPM builds. With all four fans humming, we received clearance to taxi from Pope Ground Control. With those turbines humming at 13,820 rpm, and the props turning over 1,020 rpm, you might expect the life expectancy of the brakes to be severely limited, or wonder why the 130 isn't equipped with an anchor. The answer is in the prop blades. At the taxi setting they have approximately ⅔ of their length in positive pitch, while the balance is in reverse. Nose wheel steering, through a small steering wheel located at the pilot's left knee, is used for directional control on the ground. After runup and clearance delivery, we were cleared into position and hold on the active runway. We positioned ourselves on the left side of the wide runway, while our wingman taxied into position behind and to our right.

When our takeoff clearance came, the power levers were smoothly advanced. The Herk shook and strained with the restrained power of 16,000 horses. At brake release we surged forward. Takeoff in the Herk is a two-man operation. The pilot is using the nose wheel steering with his left hand (the rudder does not become effective until 80 knots IAS), while controlling the throttles with his right. The inboard throttles are at takeoff power, while the outboards are held back. The reason for this is because, in the event of an outboard

82nd Airborne Trooper getting equipment checked by assistant jumpmaster before the jump of May 1, 1980. (Author)

'Hitting the Blast' from the Paratroop Doors (or...from the rear cargo ramp of the C-130.) (Author)

engine failure on takeoff while the opposite outboard is developing full power, nosewheel steering would not be enough to hold the airplane straight on the runway. At 80 knots, with an effective rudder, the outboards are pushed up to METO. In the meantime, the co-pilot is flying the ailerons, concentrating on keeping the wings level. (The narrow track of the main gear makes it possible to inadvertantly drop a wing enough to get the airplane going sideways.) Past 80 knots, the pilot has his hands and feet in the positions you would expect....that is, on wheel, throttles and rudders. At 105 knots he rotated and we flew off the runway smoothly.

It was a warm spring day and we were enjoying the benefit of a stable air mass....clear blue skies. But with the stable air came haze that reduced visibility to what I estimated to be about five miles. Navigation was strictly by the VFR sectional charts familiar to all Private Pilots. The intercom was alive with input from both pilots, engineer and the navigator, who was standing behind the co-pilot, pointing out ground references and relating them to our course. He scored a telling point for his navigation when, at one point, in the best tradition of navigators since time immemorial, he indicated to the pilots that our track should be "just to the left of that tree". I had to admit that he certainly didn't exhibit the cavalier attitude that troopers from my genertion had ascribed to all Air Force navigators, when it came to dropping troops on the drop zone. (We had always professed to be surprised when they got us on the drop zone, which was probably 90% of the time.) He spent a great deal of time calculating the air release point for the troops and, after the first stick had jumped, he was the first to ask where they had landed. While we were enroute the winds had picked up and were now steady at 10 knots, gusting to 15. There is nothing that will ruin an airborne operation faster than high winds. The 82nd has a policy of calling off operations if the winds exceed a steady 13 knots. In this case, everyone got onto the drop zone, apparently without undue strain.

The ride in the cockpit at 500 feet was not bad at all. There were a few bumps, but they were really hardly noticeable. But back on the ramp, between the paratroop doors, it was a different story. Totally different. It was literally impossible to maintain your feet without hanging on to something. Every thermal, every gust and every slight overcorrection on the controls was magnified unbelievably. If you didn't have a strong stomach, you were in trouble. And if you were a little nervous about leaping out of an airplane to begin with, you were a cinch to be using the plastic bags scattered throughout the cabin. Since I wasn't going to be jumping, and I do have a strong stomach, it was little more than a nuisance to me as I tried to buckle on the safety harness and arrange my cameras for easy use, but there were more than a few troopers whose faces were beginning to match their uniforms.

The difference between 500 feet and 1250 feet AGL was really amazing. Once we climbed to jump altitude and slowed down to 120 knots, the airplane became completely docile. The ritual of the jump commands was pretty much as I had remembered it, with one notable exception. The two safety jumpmasters, who would not jump, were now playing a much more active role in seeing to it that everyone's equipment was thoroughly checked. And when the time came to jump, each trooper had his static line held until after he had departed the airplane. There was simply no way that a static line was going to get entangl-ed. Another change was the metronomic pace of the troopers. While we had regularly emptied airplanes in one pass at the drop zone in the 1950s, they now took at least two passes to do the job. The reasons for this are simply for safety's sake. While the likelihood of entanglements was great with our old T-10 parachutes, they had multiplied several times over with the introduction of the controllable canopy. If that seems contradictory, you have to consider what the controllable canopy means to the parachutist. The first thing he thinks about after his parachute opens is where he is going to land. He fixes on the ground and, more often than not, will ignore the possiblity of imminent mid-air colli-sions. In a peacetime environment, where the only thing you are practicing is your jump technique, it doesn't make sense to risk the dangers of a closely packed combat drop. The exit of each jumper is now controlled on an individual basis by the jumpmaster, which en-sures the safe spacing of all jumpers.

With the last of the jumpers gone, the static lines hauled in and the doors slid shut, we headed back to Pope. There had been flashes of nostalgic reminiscence but, by and large, I found that not only were things not the same, but that I had changed too. I now identified with the airmen more than the jumpers. I envied them their day-to-day life of flying this great airplane. A quarter of a century later the Herk was still an impressive plane!

HERCULES
Orders/Deliveries by Customer
As of 31 December 1979

INTERNATIONAL	TOTAL	C-130A	C-130B	C-130E	C-130H	L-100	L-100-20	L-100-30
Abu Dhabi	2/2				2/2			
Angola								
—TAAG	2/2						2/2	
Argentina	10/10				10/10			
Australia	36/36	12/12		12/12	12/12			
Belgium	12/12				12/12			
Bolivia	2/2				2/2			
Brazil	16/16			11/11	5/5			
Cameroon	2/2				2/2			
Canada								
—Armed Forces	33/33		4/4	24/24	5/5			
—Maple Leaf Lsg.	1/1						1/1	
—Pacific Western	3/3					1/1	1/1	1/1
Chile	2/2				2/2			
Colombia	See Note							
Denmark	3/3				3/3			
Ecuador	3/3				3/3			
Egypt	20/20				20/20			
Gabon	3/3				1/1		1/1	1/1
Greece	12/12				12/12			
Indonesia	18/16		10/10		4/2			4/4
Iran	60/60			28/28	32/32			
Israel	12/12				12/12			
Italy	14/14				14/14			
Jordan	2/2				2/2			
Kuwait	2/2						2/2	
Libya	16/16				16/16			
Malaysia	9/6				9/6			
Morocco	12/12				12/12			
New Zealand	5/5				5/5			
Niger	2/2				2/2			
Nigeria	6/6				6/6			
Norway	6/6				6/6			
Pakistan (Gov't)	See Note							
—Pakistan Int'l Air	2/2					2/2		
Peru	6/6						6/6	
Philippines	5/5				3/3		2/2	
Portugal	5/5				5/5			
Saudi Arabia	41/40			9/9	32/31			
Singapore	2/0				2/0			
So. Africa (Gov't)	7/7		7/7					
—Safair	17/17							17/17
—Safmarine	1/1						1/1	
Spain	11/9				11/9			
Sudan	6/6				6/6			
Sweden	3/3			2/2	1/1			
Thailand	3/0				3/0			
Turkey	See Note							
United Kingdom	66/66				66/66			
Venezuela	7/7				7/7			
Yemen (North)	2/2				2/2			
Zaire (Gov't)	7/7				7/7			
—SCIBE	1/1							1/1
Zambia (Gov't)	3/3					3/3		
—Zambian Air Cgo	2/2					2/2		
DOMESTIC								
U.S. Government								
—Air Force:	882/882	216/216	131/131	389/389	146/146			
MAP	16/16		8/8	8/8				
Other	4/4	3/3	1/1					
—Air Nat'l Guard	16/8				16/8			
—Coast Guard	25/25		12/12	1/1	12/12			
—Marine Corps	60/60		46/46		14/14			
—Navy	17/17		11/11		6/6			
TACAMO	19/15			4/4	15/11			
U.S. (Civil)								
—Air America	1/1						1/1	
—Airlift Int'l	4/4					4/4		
—Alaska Airlines	3/3					3/3		
—Alaska Int'l Air	3/3							3/3
—Delta Air Lines	3/3					3/3		
—Flying W	2/2						2/2	
—Interior Airways	1/1						1/1	
—Nat'l A/C Lsg.	3/3					3/3		
—PLS Air Lease	1/1						1/1	
—Southern Air	2/2						2/2	
—Transamerica	7/7						3/3	4/4
TOTAL	1592/1567	231/231	230/230	488/488	565/540	21/21	26/26	31/31

Note: Hercules acquired secondhand already shown on list:
Columbia (3 C-130B), Pakistan (10 C-130B, 1 C-130E) and Turkey (8 C-130E)

Herky Nuts

The publication of the "C-130 In Action" marks the 18th **in Action** title that I have authored or co-authored. The majority of the photos and information in these books comes from private collections and it is the generosity of all the dedicated enthusiasts out there that makes them possible. I always try to let everyone know what I am working on, in order to get the contributory system working. When the word filtered out that we were doing the C-130, the response was overwhelming. Overwhelming in the amount of material donated and overwhelming in the fanatical dedication of the seemingly endless parade of Hercules 'specialists'. It's not surprising that Lockheed's Public Relations Coordinator, Joe Dabney, would have written his own book on the C-130, a very entertaining and factual account of the life and times of the Herky (**Herk: Hero of the Skies**). There have also been several other monographs devoted to the C-130, including Profile #223 by Paul St. John Turner, Warpaint Series 5 by Bob Archer, Airline Publications pictorial salute on the Herk's 25th Anniversary and, perhaps one of the most amazing, the Lockheed Hercules Production List compiled by Lars Olausson of Satenas, Sweden. The Production List enumerates and highlights the career of every C-130 built, insofar as details can be ascertained. It is in its third edition and is a must for any serious Herky Nut. (An unnecessary distinction. . .they are all serious.) Other notable Herky Nuts include my good friend and most consistent and prolific contributor, Norman E. Taylor, and Dave Davenport who may qualify as the most dedicted U.S. Nut. Dave, like Norm, is a retired USAF type. Dave makes his home in Spring Lake, NC, where he is within earshot of the whine and roar of the T-56s at Pope AFB. He is a regular contributor to the base newspaper, the Hercules Herald, with his cartoon chronicles of the Herky's on-going career. It's no accident that the last four digits of Dave's phone number are C130 and that he has a thriving small business based on sales of calendars and T-shirts emblazoned with his illustrated one-liners. All you Herky Nuts who don't already have his address can get your T-shirts by writing Dave at: Herky Bird Unlimited, P.O. Box 25, Spring Lake, NC 28390. For every Herky Nut I have mentioned here, there are dozens of others, and the list grows with the ever-widening realization that the Lockheed C-130 Hercules may be the most diverse, dependable and, if it continues in production, prolific transport ever built.

Dave Davenport and wife Maggie in the midst of their entrepreneurial realm, built on dedication to the C-130.

CENTURION in action

F-14 TOMCAT in action

U.S. SUBS in action

Jets

TIGER I in ACTION

Tanks

A-7 CORSAIR II in action

Ships

U.S. BATTLESHIP in action Part 1

squadron/signal publications WARSHIPS No.

Fighters

B-17 IN ACTION
AIRCRAFT NO. TWELVE

P-51 Mustang in action

$4.95

47221

WZ

squadron/signal publications
AIRCRAFT No. 45

Waffen SS in ACTION

Bombers

$4.95

Panzergrenadiers in ACTION

B-25 MITCHELL in action

Soldiers

squadron/signal publications
WEAPONS NUMBER FIVE

and More...

squadron/signal publications
AIRCRAFT NO. 34

squadron/signal publications